Language and Communication Difficulties

Dimitra Hartas

continuum
LONDON • NEW YORK

Continuum International Publishing Group

The Tower Building
11 York Road
London
SE1 7NX

15 East 26th Street
New York, NY 10010

British Library Cataloguing-in-Publication Data
A catalogue record for this book is available from the British Library.

ISBN: 0 8264 7614 7 (paperback)

Typeset by Servis Filmsetting Ltd, Manchester
Printed and bound in Great Britain by MPG Books Ltd, Bodmin,
Cornwall

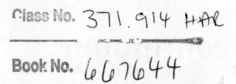

Contents

Introduction

Communicating in the classroom

Public awareness of the importance of language and communication skills for children's learning and social adjustment has grown considerably over the last years. Traditionally, language difficulties were dealt with before the child started school because they become apparent at a pre-school age. However, there is a growing understanding that the impact of language difficulties persists well into the school years, affecting both learning and social adjustment and emotional development, making the need for classroom-based language support more pressing than ever.

This book is mainly intended for teachers. Its aim is to help you, as a teacher, to gain knowledge and a practical understanding of the complexities of children's language and communication, and their contribution towards learning and social and emotional development. This book was written with an understanding of the considerable pressure on your time. Thus, the suggestions made are flexible in that they can be implemented either in a one-to-one or group situation (e.g. circle time), peer-collaborative groups where children work together, or can take place in the classroom where you work collaboratively with other professionals (e.g. classroom assistants, SENCOs).

The main premise of this book is that language and communication skills are central to human functioning, in that learning, social adjustment, emotional maturity and the development of interpersonal skills all depend upon them. For the majority of children, language develops without any concerns. By reception, as Karmiloff and her colleagues point out, most children are fully formed 'grammatical beings' capable of constructing lengthy sentences, using appropriate vocabulary and communicating complex meanings. There is a group of children, however, who do not seem to acquire language at the same rate or in the same manner as their peers. Their language development appears atypical or delayed, resulting in difficulties accessing the curriculum, learning and developing social skills.

Provision for children with language difficulties

Traditionally, children with language and communication difficulties were 'pulled out' of the classroom to receive remedial services and develop a set of language skills in the hope that these would transfer back into the classroom to support their learning. There is an ongoing criticism, however, with this type of provision, which is seen as fragmented and less effective in terms of enabling children to transfer their linguistic knowledge back into the classroom and make connections with the subject matter.

Also, up until now, language and communication difficulties were observed in the context of other conditions, being seen mostly as a secondary condition, and thus special educational provision did not target language *per se* but what was thought to be the primary condition, e.g. Asperger's syndrome, dyslexia. The majority of children who present language difficulties as a primary condition tend to receive language support during the preschool years. There is evidence to suggest that these children carry on experiencing language and communication difficulties long after language therapy has stopped, sometimes well into the adolescent years. Thus, early recognition and provision of thorough language support to meet these children's needs in the mainstream is particularly important.

Pupils' needs with regard to the development of language and communication skills can be met in the mainstream through differentiation. Although differentiation is seen as an important aspect of the National Curriculum, it is less clear to the majority of teachers as to what it entails. Many teachers and other educational practitioners understand differentiation as a process of teaching the same curriculum to all pupils and tailoring teaching methods in order to match curriculum requirements to the children's ability, prior skills and needs. Others see differentiation as a way of teaching different aspects of the curriculum to meet children's diverse needs. The latter notion of differentiation, however, is less likely to support inclusive education.

Teachers' and speech and language therapists' (SLTs) changing roles

What!

Current policies with regard to the delivery of speech and language services have introduced changes in the way SLTs work together with the teachers in schools. Specifically, regarding SLTs, there is a move towards adopting a 'consultant' role in terms of providing skills, knowledge and technical assistance to teachers, SENCOs or classroom assistants to enable them to support pupils in the mainstream. In most cases, SLTs do not serve or interact with the child with language difficulties directly but rather liaise with you, the teacher, who provides the language services/support needed.

Recently, there have been a number of governmental initiatives to support the collaborative workings between teachers and SLTs. DfES supported the charity Invalid Children's Aid Nationwide (I CAN) to develop a Joint Professional Framework for Training (Law *et al.* 2001) providing the basis for joint post-qualification training for SLTs and teachers. A joint training aims at helping you to develop a better understanding of the principles of speech and language therapy. Likewise, it is expected to raise awareness among SLTs of the constraints of the national curriculum and the demands placed on teachers, especially when faced with the challenge of teaching pupils with diverse learning profiles and needs. Law and his colleagues (2000) recommended that the curricula of initial teaching and education courses are such as to enable teachers and SLTs to work together. Establishing a comprehensive accredited system of educational and training opportunities for all child professionals who work with children with speech, language and communication needs is also expected to support interprofessional collaboration.

In this climate, there is a growing expectation for both teachers and SLTs to form good working relationships. For this collaboration to be successful, it is important to discuss and reach a consensus on the type/nature of language support provided in the mainstream, and on ways of linking it with existing curricular structures to promote effective teaching and learning (Hartas 2004). For example, when new information is discussed or expert advice is given during consultation, the content (information/skills that need to be acquired – topics), method (how we deliver the information), sequence (what to teach and in what circumstances) and the contextual, social/cultural aspects of learning should be negotiated.

Language in the mainstream

My aim in writing this book is to increase awareness about the complex needs that children with language and communication difficulties present, and discuss classroom strategies that are consistent with existing curricular structures and the framework set by the *SEN Code of Practice* (DfES 2001). The *SEN Code of Practice* is a non-statutory document that provides practical advice with regard to identifying and meeting children's special educational needs. Thus, the chapters of this book are written in a way that provides information about language development and language/ communication difficulties by discussing issues of identification, coexistence with other areas of need, the impact of language difficulties on both learning and social–emotional development and classroom practice.

For primary and secondary school pupils, the *Code of Practice* places an emphasis on classroom strategies to meet their needs effectively. It specifically states:

Language and Communication Difficulties

The key to meeting the needs of all children lies in the teacher's knowledge of each child's skills and abilities and the teacher's ability to match this knowledge with ways of providing appropriate access to the curriculum for every child. (para 5.37)

The key principles that underpin the *Code of Practice* are

♦ meeting the needs of children in the mainstream

♦ emphasis on ascertaining the views and wishes of the child with SEN (having a voice)

♦ access to a broad and balanced curriculum

♦ the importance of early identification of SEN

♦ the importance of partnership between parents and teachers/practitioners and

♦ the importance of appreciating complex factors in the educational setting

With these key principles in mind, this book is organized around the topics of language development and identification, assessment and provision for children with language and communication difficulties, either alone or in the context of other areas of need. It also discusses the interplay between language and social–emotional development and draws links between language skills and learning how to read and write. I hope that this book will help you achieve a match between children's language and communication needs and classroom practice by providing some information about the nature of language difficulties, their impact, as well as guidance on remedial strategies. I also hope that you will enjoy reading about this fascinating journey called language development.

1

Children's Language Development

Defining the territory

Communication, speech and language sound like the same thing and are often used interchangeably in our daily conversations. However, these terms mean different things, and it is important to clarify their meanings right at the start of this book.

Language is a socially shared code, a set of arbitrary symbols and rules that govern the combination of these symbols which are used to convey ideas, thoughts, emotions and intentions. These symbols and their combinations are loaded with meaning shared by a community with certain social and cultural norms and conventions. Language includes speech but it can also be written or signed. Speech involves the production and articulation of the sounds of a given language.

Communication is the broadest of all three terms, encompassing speech, language and other forms of representing experience, such as facial expressions, gestures, body language, intonation and rate of speech. Communication also requires a good knowledge of the shared norms, conventions and values of the communicative context. Competence in communicating with others requires more than linguistic skills and adequate speech articulation. Good communication skills rely heavily on having good social knowledge, a clear purpose and an understanding of the listener's needs and the demands of the conversational context.

Children's knowledge about the rules of the language is called linguistic competence, whereas their ability to use language socially refers to conversational/communicative competence. In this book the terms 'conversation' and 'communication' are used interchangeably, although it is understood that communication can be verbal as well as non-verbal. The term 'language' is defined across its five components, i.e. phonology, morphology, syntax, semantics and pragmatics. You are likely to encounter these terms in your discussions with speech and language therapists and educational psychologists, as well as in your readings about children's language development. It is important to look at children's language across these parameters or components in order to understand the pathways of language development and the type/nature of language and communication difficulties that some children experience.

The following is a brief description of language components:

♦ Phonology refers to the speech sounds of language. For example, the word 'cat' consists of three sounds, i.e. /c/, /a/, /t/. Individual sounds are called phonemes (phoneme is the smallest unit of sound).

♦ Morphology refers to the units of language that facilitate grammar and syntax. For example, the unit 's' when put at the end of nouns indicates plural or the unit '-ed' at the end of verbs indicates past tense.

♦ Syntax refers to the structure of the sentences, specifying the way words are put together, the way sentences are organized and the relationship between words and other sentence elements. For example, a syntactic rule is that a sentence should include a verb and a noun.

♦ Semantics refers to the meaning of words. The answer to the question 'What do you mean?' forms the basis of semantics. For example, the words 'learning', 'growth' and 'development' carry similar meanings, and thus they can be grouped together.

♦ Pragmatics refers to the way language is used in the social context. So, pragmatics is the communicative aspect of language. For example, taking into consideration the listener's needs (adaptation to listener's knowledge about a conversational topic) during a conversation indicates pragmatic knowledge. Also, using and understanding figurative language (e.g. metaphors, sarcasm, jokes), as well as reading 'clues' in a social setting requires good pragmatic skills.

It is understood that children become effective communicators once they have achieved competence in all these areas. Specifically, they need to know about the language forms, in terms of how words sound – phonology – and how to put them together – syntax – and how to diversify/manipulate components of words for grammar purposes – morphology. The next step is to know that these forms can be used creatively to convey meaning (knowledge of semantics). Finally, they need to understand the social conventions and norms that determine how people use language so they can appreciate intention, understand the needs of a listener and use language effectively (knowledge of pragmatics). Pragmatics, or the communicative aspect of language, goes beyond the knowledge of the structural aspects of language, i.e. phonics, syntax, grammar, to include knowledge of the social context and its cultural norms and an understanding of the conversational partner's intentions and needs. Language does not occur in a vacuum; thus, to become an effective communicator you need to understand the social/ cultural norms, previous knowledge about a conversational subject and the various reconstructions of words and meanings. Considering the inherent complexity of language, it is a miracle how easily and naturally most children acquire it during the first years of their life.

The journey to language development

Many language theorists (e.g. Karmiloff-Smith) refer to the process of language development as a 'journey' that starts in the womb and continues through childhood, adolescence and beyond. In the past, acquisition of language was thought to take place around the age of 12 months because it is around that age that we observe the first signs of language production (e.g. complex babbling, first words) in babies. Now we know that language acquisition starts way before, even before birth, although it may not be obvious and directly observable. Current research tells us that from as early as the twentieth week of gestation, the foetus's hearing system is developed sufficiently to process and react to some of the sounds that penetrate the amniotic fluid. Of course one may argue about the clarity and intelligibility of these sounds and whether they can actually trigger auditory processing in the foetus. From the sixth month of gestation the foetus processes linguistic information, and starts to recognize a mother's voice. Once outside the womb, a baby is ready to listen to human speech, being particularly attracted to his/her mother's voice.

By the time they reach the age of formal schooling, children are able to use language in a functional way to request information or an object, protest, inform and comment. They can also use language in their social interactions with both peers and adults to carry out a conversation. Engaging in a conversation is rather complex, in that children are required to bring together the social knowledge necessary to understand the listener's intention and the linguistic skills to greet, apologize and negotiate during their social interactions. They also need to apply strategies, e.g. turn-taking, repair when a communicative breakdown occurs, changing and maintaining a topic of conversation, that are required for effective communication. Furthermore, they are expected to acquire subtle communicative skills, such as communicative intent through sharing information with another person, and the ability to take the speaker's or listener's perspective by understanding their goals, intentions and beliefs. Last but not least, making sense of the use of gestures or body language when interacting face-to-face with others is instrumental in becoming a competent communicator.

Communicating in the classroom: why is it important?

The ability to communicate effectively is fundamental to all aspects of human functioning, in that thinking, learning, showing empathy, relating socially and emotionally to others and, ultimately, constructing an identity all depend upon it. Language development and the imaginative ways children use language is an exciting and important aspect of human development. It is fascinating to see it in action from early childhood settings to primary and secondary school classrooms. Most children develop language without any problems. However, there is a group of children for whom the understanding and use of language is a perpetual struggle across contexts, from the playground, to the classroom, to the family/community settings.

Communicating in the classroom can be particularly challenging, especially for children with language difficulties. As Cazden (1988) argues, classrooms are complex and crowded social environments where talking and listening serve many purposes, such as responding to teacher's questioning, narrating an event, participating in a discussion and engaging in collaborative group learning with other classmates, to mention a few. In most classrooms the conversational emphasis is placed on responding to teacher-initiated questions, with limited time given to free discussions for the purpose of exploring ideas and talking about feelings. The latter is likely to occur in a circle time setting (discussed in detail in Chapters 3 and 4), where children are encouraged to converse not only with the teacher but also with each other. Children with communication difficulties, however, tend to engage in limited conversational inter-actions with both teachers and peers, often expecting others to carry the weight of the conversation. Thus, placed in a classroom with rigid communication rules and procedures, they are likely to be disadvantaged and miss a great deal of the knowledge generated through classroom discussions.

Moreover, the use of language in the classroom is demanding, given that children are encouraged to talk about events that are not 'here and now' and not experienced by those who are present. For example, when children are asked to tell a story about an event or an experience that occurs outside the classroom, it places a lot of linguistic and communicative demands and pressures on them. For some young children, starting to use language in an abstract way is an uneasy transition from the 'here-and-now' type of language they normally use in their family context where there is face-to-face conversation, gesture and a known audience to repair communication break-downs and support meaning-making.

The *Curriculum Guidance for the Foundation Stage* (DfEE/QCA 2000) has recognized the importance of developing good language and communication skills, with a particular emphasis given in pre-school settings. It is important for teachers to become aware of chil-dren's language needs as early as possible to ensure that appropriate support is given.

The Early Learning Goals places emphasis on the importance of pupils:

♦ interacting with others, negotiating plans and activ-ities and taking turns in conversations

♦ listening to and using spoken and written language

♦ sustaining attentive listening, responding to what they have heard by relevant comments, questions or actions

♦ listening with enjoyment and responding to stories, songs and other music, rhymes and poems, and making up their own stories, songs, rhymes and poems

♦ expanding their vocabulary, exploring the meanings and sounds of new words

♦ speaking clearly and audibly with confidence and control and showing awareness of the listener, for example by use of conventions such as greetings, 'please' and 'thank you'

♦ using language to imagine and recreate roles and experiences, and

♦ using speech to organize, sequence and clarify thinking, ideas, feelings and events

(DfEE/QCA 2000: 48–59)

It is interesting to see how central language is with regard to the learning goals for young children. Although the National Curriculum stresses the importance of speaking and listening skills in children as a prerequisite for literacy development, it focuses on 'English' rather than 'language' or 'languages' or 'other languages'. With regard to the last, I will be discussing the learning and social experiences of children who speak English as a second language in Chapter 5.

Scaffolding communication

Vygotsky (1962) has argued that learning takes place within the context of social interactions where children share responsibility for relating meaningfully to adult and peers. In this case, the role of the adult is seen as being facilitative, giving as much assistance as is needed while, over time, the child will become increasingly confident and able to function independently. The metaphorical term 'scaffolding', used by Bruner (1987) and his colleagues, has come to apply to a social interaction of this kind. This model can be used successfully to support pupils in developing communication skills, especially those with difficulties in this area who are also less confident in practising newly acquired language skills.

Children's communication can be enhanced through scaffolding, which basically means to assist children during the process of learning and practising language and communication skills. You, as a teacher, as well as other more conversationally competent pupils, can provide the support to help children with language and communication difficulties in particular to develop the skills necessary to express ideas, generate solutions to a problem, participate in classroom discussions and influence each others' social behaviour.

Scaffolding is a form of reciprocal teaching in which both the teacher and the pupils are involved. Probably most of you use scaffolding during your daily classroom routines without even realizing it. For example, during storytelling some of you may scaffold a pupil narrating a story by asking a number of questions and drawing links between ideas, events or situations.

Specifically, you may even repeat the last sentence or words the child has said to make a connection or ask 'What happened next?' Asking 'wh' questions about the setting and the main characters of the story has been found to support pupils' attempts to elaborate on the characters' feelings, thoughts and intentions. Finally, you may probe into information that is not clear or needs elaboration, or supply the next piece of information to help the child move further. All these scaffolding strategies can be easily integrated into the natural flow of storytelling in the classroom and support children's narratives.

Other ways of scaffolding are by reformulating the questions in order to reduce their linguistic burden and by using expansions. For example, instead of asking a child who narrates a story 'what are the character's [Lucy's] intentions' you may ask him/her, 'What's Lucy going to do next?' Also using expansions by extending or elaborating further on a very simple and restricted sentence produced by a child can be particularly helpful for young children and those with language difficulties who are likely to find storytelling as well as other types of spontaneous speech particularly challenging.

Storytelling and narratives differ from dialogues in that conversations, especially among children, always contain cues from the 'here and now' so they can easily ascertain the subject of a conversation. Narratives, on the other hand, cannot rely on these cues. The narrator needs to sequence and organize a number of sentences together in a way that makes sense and relates to the listener. He/she has to take into consideration the listener's background knowledge with regard to the event narrated and to be both coherent and cohesive. Coherence refers to the way the topic of the narrative holds together, and cohesion refers to the linguistic devices, e.g. grammar, syntax, employed to link sentences together.

It is a balancing act for some teachers to 'scaffold' conversations in the classroom and not monopolize them by engaging in lengthy discussions or exam-type questions, especially when interacting with children whose language use is restricted. It pays dividends to be flexible and accommodating in the way you interact with pupils with language difficulties. Classroom observations reveal that when teachers ask pupils questions, they typically wait for one second or less for them to start replying and then react to their answers directly after the pupils have finished before moving on to the next question. In this type of interaction, there is limited opportunity for using language creatively to elaborate and explore ideas further.

A fundamental question that you may ask is whether your classroom is language-rich, not only in terms of the number of activities that promote language use but, most importantly, whether they send a message that you are nurturing a community of speakers and listeners. As Whitehead (2002) argues, there are many ways to make language exposure and experimentation in the classroom possible and encourage pupils to practise and consolidate newly acquired language and communication skills. Specifically, you can create opportunities for conversational exchanges by giving detailed verbal instructions, reciting poetry and engaging children in 'listening walks', where they can go outside the classroom to collect interesting sounds and then come back in the classroom and share them with their classmates.

Also, there is a plethora of resources, e.g. audiotapes, music CDs, rhymes that children can listen to and sing along with, that you can use, as well as activities such as drama, role-playing, storytelling and daily discussions about the everyday planning of a classroom that can support language development.

In today's educational climate, it is particularly challenging, and somewhat unrealistic, to create language-rich classrooms, considering that teachers are expected to communicate effectively with 35 or more children who present various degrees of abilities and needs. Teachers are also expected to work effectively within the rigid structure and the constraints that the National Curriculum poses. However, it is important, as much as possible, to be less prescriptive and adopt a genuinely conversational approach in your interactions with children by avoiding 'test questions' in which only one answer is correct, and allow for more exploratory talk to engage in joint meaning-making with pupils.

What does it take to become a good communicator?

Language does not occur in isolation; thus when we are thinking about ways of communicating in the classroom we need to take into consideration the physical, social and psychological dimensions of the classroom itself. Classrooms that are predictable and safe environments, supportive of children's motivation and self-image and reflective of caregivers' and children's preferences are conducive to language development and learning.

With regard to the psychological–social aspects of

classroom interactions, children's motivation and preferences should be respected by documenting them and taking them into account when planning activities. Social motivation plays a significant role in enhancing language and communication skills. Some children may find communicating stressful, or may communicate only during a limited number of activities. In addition to their interests, activities should be designed to take into consideration children's developmental strengths and learning styles, as well as their early linguistic experiences with their families. Many children with language difficulties present uneven profiles and may have unique learning styles and early learning experiences.

For many decades, language theorists and practitioners considered language to be a subset of skills that can be learned through reinforcement and modelling from parents or other adults. Behaviourists thought that language develops through a sequence of stimulus and response, with longer sentences being learned through imitation. For example, when a child says the word 'mummy' to his mother, the mother reinforces it with her attention or with a comment she makes. In this case, mother's presence is the stimulus to elicit the child's responses. This approach to language development has not been very helpful, in that it does not take into account the richness of social interactions, the emotional aspects of caregiver–child relationships and the important role that social/cultural practices play in language development. Over the last decades, we have gradually moved away from this notion of teaching and learning language and communication skills to a more holistic and context-based understanding of language development.

Children's Language Development

For children to develop good communication skills, they need to be aware and able to respond to a number of conversational demands, such as turn-taking, topic-maintenance, making requests and repairing communicative breakdowns. These lay the foundations for successful communication. Specifically, turn-taking, which can be both verbal and non-verbal, is important in order to avoid rude interrupting, calling out or being quiet. Linguistically, turn-taking requires the ability to understand non-verbal cues (e.g. gestures, facial expressions), comprehend linguistic rules (e.g. grammar, syntax) and become aware of when and how the rules shift in order to respond rapidly.

Topic-maintenance requires the ability to initiate and respond in a way that is relevant and meaningful to the ongoing conversation, as opposed to making inappropriate comments, interrupting or asking many questions and disturbing the natural flow of a conversation. Linguistically, a child needs to be able to identify a topic, formulate and retrieve appropriate vocabulary, repair and clarify when necessary, use comments to expand and rephrase, comprehend and use humour.

Making requests (e.g. attention, objects, actions, information, clarification) appropriately by using verbal and non-verbal behaviours (gestures and facial expression), as opposed to yelling, walking away, grabbing, giving up, being impulsive and jumping to conclusions. Requests are particularly important when they take place for clarification purposes to avoid a possible communication breakdown. Linguistically, to make requests properly, a child requires good expressive vocabulary, comprehension of words and sentences (receptive vocabulary), ability to 'read between the lines' and figure out implicit messages and skills to match old with new information and identify 'gaps' that need clarification or repair.

Working in partnership with parents

Language and communication skills can and should be supported outside the classroom, in children's family and community settings. You should talk with parents and collaborate with them to ensure consistency and transference of the linguistic support given in the classroom. Developing good partnerships with parents and carers is particularly important if you work with young children with communication difficulties. The most important language and communication experiences for the majority of children occur in their family. Therefore, the family context, e.g. beliefs and values of the family, and patterns of interaction among family members, all need to be taken into consideration when discussing strategies to support the development of communication skills. Working closely with families to achieve a consistency and continuity with regard to the provision of language and communication support is not as easy as one might think. You need to understand various family practices and functions and how they are influenced by ethnic, social and economic factors. The parents' perspective on their children's communication and language development may be different from that held by you. Thus it is important to clarify expectations and understandings about children's language profiles by focusing on strengths and weaknesses.

As already stressed above, it is good practice to involve parents when supporting young children with language and communication difficulties. One way of doing that is by discussing with them a number of strategies that they can carry out at home to help their children's language. These strategies should focus on:

♦ Developing 'shared attention', especially for those children who present difficulties with listening, attending and regulating their emotions and behaviour. For example, call the child's name before talking to him/her or use a visual display to facilitate attention and make connections to the things said.

♦ Encouraging a two-way communication for those with difficulties in social reciprocity. This can be achieved by demonstrating turn-taking and modelling responses for greeting, requesting clarification and using language politely.

♦ Explaining that language is used to share meanings with other people to help children understand that language is a symbolic system. During role-playing or a dilemma situation, for example, you can show how language is used to influence others and set the stage for events to take place by generating solutions and enacting them.

♦ Facilitating and modelling ways that language can be used to support emotional thinking and responding by integrating feelings and thoughts and using language to express emotions. This is normally achieved by teaching children to use emotion words, not only those that describe basic emotions (e.g. happy, sad) but also complex feelings such as embarrassment, guilt, etc.

Working with parents collaboratively can strengthen your classroom work by creating more opportunities for children to practise newly acquired language and communication skills in their natural setting (i.e. family, community) where at the same time they are assisted by their caregivers.

Summary

In this chapter I defined the territory of language and communication development and stressed the importance of children becoming effective communicators and engaging in classroom discussions. It appears that the answer to the question of what it takes to become a good communicator is not straightforward. Language is a complex behaviour, affected by many factors (e.g. early linguistic and social experiences, family/community social and economic structures, degree of exposure to language, value placed on language learning) that are above and beyond your control as a teacher. However, simple strategies that can be embedded in the curricular structure of your classroom can make a huge difference in helping children to become good communicators and successful and independent learners.

2

Language and Communication Difficulties

Language profiles and needs

I would like to start this chapter by presenting a case-study of a child who experiences language and communication difficulties. If you look around in your classroom, you will most certainly find children who fit the profile of needs described here.

Joe is a physically active child who enjoys playing alone or with younger children. His parents describe him as a quiet boy who follows what his siblings do. They said that he reached all the developmental milestones in time, except for speech and language, being described as a 'late talker'. His mother also remembers that, as a toddler, Joe did not engage in pretend play in terms of making stories while he was playing with his toys. By the time he entered primary school he was exhibiting limitations in his language and communication skills in terms of sharing stories, providing answers to simple questions and following instructions, making requests, using language socially (e.g. greeting) and engaging in problem-solving. At school, his teachers noted that he rarely speaks during whole-class discussions and collaborative learning activities. They also noted that he has difficulties understanding and applying grammar and syntax, in particular during reading and writing. Moreover, his vocabulary was said to be immature and inaccurate at times, using simple, 'babyish', words. In the playground, he does not interact with his peers; he would rather be with younger children. During games, he seems somewhat lost, either following what other children do or doing irrelevant things. During peer-group interactions he does not wait for his turn, resulting in either interrupting others or not talking at all. At times he gets frustrated when he tries to get a message across unsuccessfully.

This case-study illustrates the ways in which difficulties with language and communication affect learning, social and interpersonal interaction and emotional development. Joe does not have the linguistic tools to participate in classroom discussions, play with other children, initiate conversations with them, tell stories and follow instructions. Also, because of lack of language skills, he gets easily frustrated and is likely to display behavioural difficulties (e.g. throwing tantrums). Joe's learning is likely to suffer greatly in that his limited language skills do not allow him to access the curriculum fully and comprehensively.

It is apparent from Joe's profile that, to engage in conversations successfully, children must segment the stream of speech into meaningful units and then put them back together into meaningful chunks by taking the context into account. By engaging in this process they build language skills that are both receptive (understanding) and expressive (communication). For most children this is a straightforward process, but for others, it is a perpetual struggle, mainly because they experience difficulties that can be traced in the form–meaning relationship, i.e. the interaction between language form, content and use. These difficulties are likely to underlie every aspect of language. Specifically, with phonological segmentation, a child has to segment sentences, even one-word utterances, into meaning-relevant chunks. From a very early age, children learn to detect cues to segmentation and word boundaries. Karmiloff-Smith and her colleagues pointed out that infants show sensitivity to rhythmic patterns and syllable sequence, and can register complex prosodic features of speech to enable them with segmentation (Karmiloff and Karmiloff-Smith, 2002).

Defining language and communication difficulties

In the previous chapter, I defined communication as encompassing a variety of skills, such as the ability to produce and comprehend speech/sounds, apply grammatical and syntactical rules and understand the cues of the social context. I also stressed that children need to acquire both linguistic and social knowledge in order to become effective communicators. Children's understanding of the context and the connections between the context and speech is essential for making meaning. For example, a child might focus his/her attention on an element of the environment to which a word refers. This acts as a prompt to find words that correspond to this element. Ideally, both the child and his/her caregiver will direct their attention to the same object or event and make the connection between what they see and the speech they hear, in a process called 'joint attention'. Children with language

Language and Communication Difficulties

and communication difficulties, however, appear to experience problems with the form of language (sounds, grammar and syntax); the content of language (semantics or meaning); and the social function of language (pragmatics or communication) in any combination and in terms of expressive and receptive aspects of language.

[Language and communication difficulties refer to a wide array of problems with the use and understanding of language.] These include difficulties producing grammatically correct speech, ranging from dropping the articles to putting words together randomly; limited capacity in retrieving words that are already known; disturbances in the voluntary production of speech in that one may be able to articulate a word in the natural flow of speech but cannot pronounce it when asked to do so; and difficulties with deriving meaning from language, written or oral.

The academic and social implications of language difficulties seem to persist many years after the difficulty is remedied. There is research showing that children with language and communication difficulties show changes in the type and severity of their problems over the years, with subtle communication problems persisting into adolescence and adulthood. Also, it has been shown that, in some cases, certain language problems are not detected up until middle childhood, when language becomes more demanding. Indeed, as they approach adolescence, children are expected to be able to narrate complex stories, reason and engage in arguments, interpret implicit messages and figurative speech (e.g. metaphors, irony) and interact socially in a variety of social settings.

Is Joe's language 'atypical'?

There has been an ongoing debate among educators and other child professionals into what is considered to be atypical language. What does 'atypical' mean? Does the term refer to a 'deviant' or a 'delayed' pattern of language development? Why is it important to make this distinction? The truth is that it is difficult to draw precise boundaries between typical and atypical patterns of language development. There are many reasons to explain the lack of clarity when it comes to identifying language difficulties.

First, there is a huge variability with regard to the onset of language in children, and this does not help us to differentiate between language delay and language difficulty with accuracy. For example, some researchers (e.g. Ingram) state that no speech at 18 months may be a sign of language difficulties, whereas others (e.g. Stackhouse *et al.* 2004) state that unintelligible speech at school entry is a more valid indication of language difficulties. Some children form their first words between 18 and 24 months of age, whereas others start somewhat later. Nevertheless, by the age of 5, both early and late developers almost certainly speak fluently, although their language development is far from complete (Karmiloff and Karmiloff-Smith 2002).

Secondly, difficulties with differential diagnosis can be explained by considering the limitations of current assessment devices and procedures. There are two main assessment procedures put in place to identify language difficulties, i.e. qualitative and quantitative. A quantitative assessment normally involves the use of standardized tests that give you the normative standing (a numerical score) of an individual child compared to the performance of all the children of his/her age. There is an ongoing criticism with regard to the validity of these tests in that they tend to favour monolingual speakers, cannot be used with very young children due to lack of early-years norms and, most importantly, are seen as reducing language, a complex behaviour, into discrete sets of skills.

Standardized tests are normally used to assess skills with regard to the structure of language (e.g. phonology, syntax, grammar); however, assessing children who experience difficulties with the communicative aspect of language is more complicated than assessing specific aspects of the structure of language, with the former requiring a qualitative approach. Qualitatively, communication skills can be assessed by collecting a sample of language as it happens spontaneously in different contexts, e.g. classroom, playground, and analysing it across certain communicative skills, such as topic-maintenance, turn-taking, making requests, to mention a few.

Finally, another issue with regard to language assessment is an apparent lack of a consensus among practitioners with respect to the definitions used and the decisions on what aspects of language (e.g. phonology, syntax, grammar, semantics or pragmatics) we should focus. All these factors, and perhaps many more, contribute to the variability of current estimates of language and communication difficulties, with some studies referring to two per cent and others to seven per cent of children displaying some form of speech and language/communication difficulties.

Does Joe display Specific Language Impairment (SLI)?

There is a group of children who, although they have reached all the developmental milestones on time, experience difficulties with the development of language. These children are thought to display Specific Language Impairment. The way that SLI is defined is exclusionary in that it tells us what SLI is not rather than what it is. Specifically, SLI is thought 'not to be caused by hearing loss; general learning difficulties; environmental factors and emotional problems' (Lees and Urwin 1997: 14).

A closer look at children with SLI reveals that they have a family history of specific language difficulties, a mismatch between their language skills and other abilities and a failure to catch up despite being given 'generalized' help in the classroom and at home (Frederickson and Cline 2002). Looking for a mismatch between language and other skills had encouraged the use of the discrepancy criterion to diagnose SLI in children. Specifically, a comparison takes place between language skills and other cognitive areas, such as memory, verbal/non-verbal reasoning, to ascertain whether there is a significant gap between language and other cognitive skills. The validity of this diagnostic procedure, however, is questionable, stressing the need to move towards more developmental assessment procedures that will enable us to examine children's language in wider social and educational contexts.

Research suggests that about five per cent of children with language difficulties present SLI, which is a difficulty exclusively affecting language acquisition

Language and Communication Difficulties

(Karmiloff and Karmiloff-Smith 2002). Specifically, they present difficulties with grammar and syntax primarily, following instructions, developing a good vocabulary and participating in classroom discussions. The main problems experienced by children with SLI include understanding and applying grammatical rules, and understanding and using vocabulary. The following is a list of characteristics/behaviours that these children are likely to display. They

♦ have difficulty following conversations

♦ make serious grammatical errors when speaking or writing

♦ have difficulties understanding words that make logical connection, such as 'because', 'however', 'although', etc.

♦ have poor auditory memory, i.e. memorizing verbally presented information

♦ have difficulties talking in complete sentences, making many false starts, and

♦ appear unable to follow instructions, especially those that involve many steps

(Beveridge and Conti-Ramsden 1987)

If you are aware of a child displaying some or all of these characteristics, it is important to raise the alarm and refer the child for a speech and language assessment. To give you a flavour of the extent and the type of language difficulties that children with SLI experience I include an extract taken from Karmiloff and

Karmiloff-Smith (2002: 190) about a 14-year-old with SLI who repeats a story that has just been told:

> 'Yesterday jump in river . . . uhm . . . get new shoe . . . shoe wet. Mummy cross. Her looking for brother. Her go every-where . . . uhm . . . not find him. Hide behind tree . . . uhm . . . very naughty.'

Reading this, you would think that the above paragraph was produced by a very young child, certainly not by a 14-year-old. It is not coherent and the grammatical and syntactical rules are applied incorrectly. Also, the use of vocabulary is simplistic and the meanings expressed are not clear.

The profile of language needs presented by children with SLI is diverse. A subgroup of children with SLI are likely to present difficulties with receptive language (e.g. understanding words, meanings, verbal associa-tions). There is also a group of children who appear to have acquired language properly in that they speak flu-ently in syntactically correct sentences, but they have difficulty communicating because their conversation lacks clarity and cohesion. Supporting the latter group of children in the classroom is not easy in that they tend to experience a great deal of frustration from failing to communicate with others.

Language difficulties and other areas of need

In Joe's case, he experiences language difficulties that do not coexist with any other conditions. It is common, however, to see language difficulties in the context of other needs, either as a primary or a secondary condition, although determining causal links is not always possible. Locating children's language use in the context of other areas of need, e.g. dyslexia, dyspraxia, Asperger's syndrome and hearing impairments, has important practical implications for teaching and learning. For example, providing language support to a child with Asperger's syndrome (autistic spectrum disorder: high functioning autism) should differ dramatically in its nature, intensity, objectives and outcomes from the language support given to a child with hearing difficulties or a child with specific learning difficulties.

Specific learning difficulties (dyslexia, dyspraxia)

Children with dyslexia, a specific learning difficulty, normally present difficulties with the phonological aspect of language in terms of understanding, manipulating and articulating the sounds of language and their combinations. They also present serious difficulties with reading, at word and sentence level. The relevance of the contribution of speaking and listening to the development of reading skills has been recognized by the National Curriculum which suggests a number of language-based strategies to extract meaning from text, including supporting children to apply grammatical, syntactic and phonological knowledge to recognize words and facilitate comprehension. It has been suggested that there is variability in the way teachers view phonics, and the emphasis they place on the link between phonological development and reading and writing.

There is a subgroup of children with dyslexia who also experience SLI, presenting teachers with many challenges in that language difficulties pose additional obstacles to reading and writing. Teaching reading by taking a linguistic approach makes sense if you consider that reading and language are closely connected. The Department for Education and Employment (1998: 8) has advocated a number of language-based strategies to support literacy. Specifically,

♦ Demonstration: teach the use of phonics and pronunciation during reading and show relationships between grammar, syntax and meaning

♦ Modelling: discuss aspects of text and the processes involved in understanding it

♦ Scaffolding: offer clarifications, discuss the purpose of text and raise awareness of the different sections/aspects of a text (e.g. events, characters)

♦ Questioning: this is interactive teaching in that you offer children the opportunity to ask you or their peers questions about the text, offer opinion, make comments and inferences and draw conclusions

♦ Engaging in a debate by encouraging students to build arguments, reason, expand themes and make connection with previous knowledge

Dyspraxia, or developmental dyspraxia as it is formally called, is also a specific learning difficulty that is characterized by poor gross and fine motor coordination, difficulties with speech articulation and language and the display of immature social/emotional skills. Language difficulties are not the first characteristic that you normally think about when you encounter children with dyspraxia, in that the main area of concern is their coordination and perceptual organization. Nevertheless, their language suffers in terms of poor articulation and limited expressive language skills (verbal dyspraxia). Also, children with dyspraxia are likely to present difficulties with grammar and syntax, and the acquisition and understanding of words that denote spatial awareness and orientation (e.g. up/down, in/out, underneath). The majority of these children receive speech and language therapy before they attend school. Indeed, during their early years, they display poor articulation with speech, in some cases with being intelligible. Children with dyspraxia are also likely to display communication difficulties in terms of knowing when to take their turn during a conversation, maintaining a topic of conversation and requesting clarification.

Asperger's syndrome

Children with autistic-spectrum disorders (e.g. Asperger's syndrome) display difficulties in three areas of functioning, namely social interactions, communication (speech that is often repetitive/echolalic, idiosyncratic, abnormal intonation – high pitch) and a restricted pattern of behaviour and interests (e.g. playing with their toys in a repetitive fashion). The onset and the diagnosis of autistic-spectrum difficulties usually take place before or around the third year of age. It is a disorder of communication or the social function of language, rather than of the structure of language.

Children with what is called classic autism (that amounts to almost 50 per cent of children with autistic-spectrum disorders) experience cognitive delays and do not develop language. However, children with Asperger's syndrome do develop language, albeit with serious difficulties in the communicative aspect of language, manifested in terms of difficulties deciphering social cues, taking the listener's perspective, contributing relevant information to a conversation, maintaining a topic and engaging in different functions of language, e.g. greeting, commenting. Regarding classroom support, you as a teacher need to be aware of their language and communication delays, particularly in learning vocabulary and grammar, and engaging in classroom discussions. Thus, reading materials need to be within the child's understanding and experience to ensure comprehension, and also should be presented by using multiple modalities, i.e. visual, verbal.

Hearing impairment

There are three types of hearing difficulties known, i.e. conductive, sensorineural and mixed (Frederickson and Cline 2002). Conductive refers to the breakdown of the system that conducts the sound to the inner ear. Ear infections are the most common cause of conductive loss. Normally, this type of hearing difficulty is not severe and can be fixed by inserting grommets. Sensorineural involves damage to the inner ear and that is more difficult to treat, resulting in complete hearing loss. In the last decades, advances in medicine have introduced a surgical procedure that involves cochlea implants as a means of recovering. This procedure has generated a great deal of controversy among communities of deaf individuals who perceive their condition not as a deficit that can be medically fixed but as part of their social identity, of who they are. These diametrically opposing points of view with regard to deafness have informed the current debate on deaf children's language development and learning, and have raised questions as to whether teaching and learning through sign language constitute a form of bilingual education. It has been found that, within a deaf family where sign language is used, deaf babies normally develop a form of manual babbling. Within a hearing family, mothers talk to their deaf children as much as they do to their hearing children, and are likely to use visual cues to facilitate communication. Nevertheless, opportunities for incidental learning are reduced in deaf children.

In your classroom, you probably have encountered or will encounter children with mild to moderate hearing difficulties which, if not diagnosed at a pre-school stage, have most likely affected language development. Obviously, the degree of language and communication impairment varies according to the degree of hearing loss. Usually, children with hearing impairment experience difficulties with both language and cognitive development (e.g. thinking, perceiving, understanding). Linguistically, with regard to understanding and producing sounds, the vowels are affected. Also, syntactic and semantic development is normal but greatly delayed. Communication difficulties are present, especially as children enter school: they have difficulty learning the rules that govern classroom discussions, interacting with other children meaningfully, following instructions and working independently.

We all agree that classrooms are crowded and noisy environments with many distractions, certainly not conducive to learning for a child with hearing difficulties. Hearing difficulties, especially at a mild–moderate range, can be easily missed. There are certain characteristics that children with hearing difficulties are likely to display and, although some of them overlap with those presented by children with either learning or attention difficulties, they can be very helpful in identifying children with hearing difficulties.

The following list of behaviours associated with hearing loss has been adapted from Webster and Wood (1989) and Watson (1996). You should certainly raise the issue of hearing difficulties and obtain information about the child's developmental history from the parents if you encounter a pupil in your classroom who

♦ is often slow to react to instructions or repeatedly asks what to do although he/she has been told

♦ watches others to see what they do and then follows

♦ constantly asks others to repeat what they have said

♦ hears sometimes and not others, especially if he/she stands at one specific point in the room

♦ is unable to locate a speaker or the source of sound

♦ has a tendency to daydream or shows poor concentration, especially during group instructions or when a story is read aloud

♦ makes inappropriate comments as though he/she has not follow the topic of conversation

♦ has delayed language development, e.g. immature syntax, limited vocabulary

♦ finds it difficult to repeat words or sounds or remember names

♦ sometimes shouts without realizing this

♦ misses consonants from the end of words

♦ confuses words that sound similar (fat, that)

♦ fixes eyes in the speaker as though he/she is lip-reading, and

♦ has frequent coughs and colds

Assessing language difficulties

The importance of early identification and early diagnosis of language and communication difficulties is stressed by much current research (e.g. Frederickson and Cline 2002) as well as official guidelines by the Department for Education (1994). There are several approaches to assessment, with most recent attempts focusing on children's language as occurring in natural contexts and situations.

Traditionally, standardized language assessments have been used to assess language and communication difficulties in children. A normal procedure has been to refer children with language and communication difficulties to be assessed by a speech and language therapist. The use of standard assessment devices was thought to have many advantages in that they provide an objective analysis of language use, allowing comparisons to be made between language and other cognitive areas. However, as mentioned before, there has been an ongoing criticism with regard to the validity of standardized assessments and the extent to which they inform classroom practice. As mentioned in the Introduction, the role of SLTs is gradually changing and, with that, your role with regard to supporting children's language and communication development undergoes major changes.

Teachers have always relied on qualitative assessments of children's language and communication skills. There is a growing consensus among language professionals that in order to assess children's ability to use language to construct meaning (semantics) and to communicate with others (pragmatics), a naturalistic assessment is required to allow recording of children's language as it occurs in their everyday activities and interactions. In this context, once you are aware that there are some concerns with a child's language, the next step is to collect language samples from different conversational occasions. You can then assess children's communication skills across different contexts, e.g. classroom, playground, and obtain rich and context-specific information about how they use language in their social interactions.

With regard to a qualitative approach to language assessment, storytelling and narratives provide the means to elicit language and analyse it across many communicative aspects, such as initiating and maintaining a topic, using emotion vocabulary, using functional and social language, negotiating, generating solutions to a problem, and many more. Then through a process called discourse analysis you can see whether children

- provide significant information to the listener (background information)

- use vague words

- engage in informational redundancy

- need repetition

- maintain topic

- understand the social conventions of participants

- ask relevant questions

- have inappropriate speech styles

- have difficulties with turn-taking, and

- apply problem-solving skills (e.g. generate advice, provide alternatives to resolve conflict, negotiate, evaluate advice)

Storytelling, as an assessment tool, can be used with children who do not present serious language and communication difficulties so they are capable of producing spontaneous samples of language. However, for children who experience serious difficulties and/or are young, an elicited language sample is more reasonable to obtain. Elicited language samples can be collected through the use of puppets during role-playing, or by asking children to recall personal experiences, giving them the opportunity to talk about their interests.

It is important to note that children's language should be sampled across different contexts with which they are familiar, and also language should relate meaningfully to the situation and the child's experiences and interests. Given the time constraints that you as a teacher experience, collecting and transcribing lengthy language samples is not very realistic. However, by using a pocket tape recorder you can easily collect children's language during role-playing or in the playground, and also make brief notes about the context and the activity. This exercise is quite informative with regard to children's communication skills, in that by analysing their language samples you are in the position to comment on

♦ the range and variety of communicative functions they express, such as requests for clarification or an object, greeting/apologizing, using language politely

♦ the way they initiate a topic and the relevance and meaningfulness of their responses to others

♦ changes in the use of language as a result of taking into account the context and activity, and

♦ the way they respond to their listener's needs

Summary

For the majority of children, language develops without any concern. Indeed, by the age of 4 or 5 most children are fully formed 'linguistic beings' capable of understanding and using language in novel and imaginative ways. However, for some children, language is a perpetual struggle and this has serious implications for their learning and social skills development. In this chapter, I talked about language and communication difficulties and their manifestations, either alone or in the context of other areas of need (i.e. specific learning difficulties, Asperger's syndrome and hearing impairment). Finally, I raised issues about language assessment and the developmental appropriateness of using standardized assessment tools, arguing that a qualitative approach to assessing language is more appropriate and informative for classroom practice.

3

Tackling Language and Communication Difficulties

Classroom practice

I would like to start the discussion about classroom practice by providing a general framework adapted from Webster and Wood (1989) to guide the implementation of conversational strategies in the classroom. According to this framework, you may coach children's communication by

♦ showing an interest in their play and using it as a pretext to encourage them to comment on it

♦ encouraging them to talk about events or describe absent objects, modelling the use of language to describe 'there-and-then' situations

♦ giving them enough time to respond as well as plenty of opportunities to engage in discussions with their peers

♦ practising language within naturally occurring events and situations

♦ clarifying and elaborating on the comments they make, and

♦ setting the physical environment of the classroom (e.g. circle time) to support dialogue and spontaneous conversation

Most of the strategies presented in this chapter have been found to be conducive to supporting children's language and communication development. They do not require any special preparation and can be adopted flexibly across curriculum, as well as during unstructured activities in the classroom or the playground. As I have already discussed in Chapter 1, forming language-rich classrooms is not easy. There is a lot of pressure placed on using your time and resources effectively and thus, it is important that the conversational strategies presented here can be embedded in the everyday curriculum.

Communication and language strategies should also be embedded, as much as possible, in naturally occurring events in the classroom or playground. It is important to follow children's interests and attention and seize opportunities to communicate and teach language within the context of social interaction. For young children, language should be used in the same way as in child–caregiver interactions (e.g. giving them time and opportunity to express their views, reformulating their incomplete sentences, using toys or visual aids to support conversation). This is particularly helpful in making language familiar and relevant to children's experiences, hopefully maximizing the potential for generalizing their skills across contexts.

Developing a deep understanding of the children's needs and interests will help you to introduce language-boosting activities that are relevant to their life experiences. This can make communication strategies easily accessible and applicable in the classroom, and also help you create opportunities for social interactions between children and other adults, e.g. classroom assistants or 'talking partners' in the classroom and playground. Certain tasks, e.g. role-playing, dilemma, referential tasks, as well as classroom structures, e.g. circle time, cooperative group learning, structured playing, facilitate language/communication and social interactions among children.

Language and communication strategies

The following strategies are expected to support all children to become competent communicators, particularly those who experience language difficulties in an inclusive setting. These strategies encompass a variety of communication skills, and can be effective if they are implemented in a context where adult assistance is readily available. They can be used with all children in an inclusive classroom, and can be easily differentiated to meet the needs of children with language and communication difficulties. There is evidence to suggest that language/communication support is effective when it is relevant to the curriculum and children's learning needs and experiences.

Traditionally, children were 'pulled out' of the classroom and were given specialist support to develop specific linguistic skills that were not always easily transferred in the classroom. The tasks suggested here can take place within the existing curriculum framework and be part of the daily classroom instruction. For example, during History or English, children may be given a hypo-thetical conflict scenario or dilemma to discuss. Or, during Art and Design, a referential task can take place to teach certain communication skills. The following tasks are designed to scaffold the learning of a variety of language and communication skills in children from as young as reception age.

Referential task

In this task, children are given the tools to repair communicative breakdowns by encouraging them to request more information from a conversational part-ner who gives an ambiguous message. Children are encouraged to recognize an informative from a non-informative or partially informative message and to use language to request more information or clarification. They may start by giving descriptions, as informative and detailed as possible, of an abstract design/figure so that the other child can identify and draw it without seeing it. There are many variations to this task. You may also ask children to identify and pick one figure from a number of figures in a box, and draw it by hand or by using a computer. Certain communication skills such as paraphrasing and revising unclear messages can be demonstrated, encouraged and practised during this task.

Role-playing

Role-playing is very effective in teaching and practising certain communication skills, such as social problem-solving, conveying positive and negative messages and addressing the listener's needs. For example, you may ask children to give negative feedback to an imaginary peer during hypothetical situations, and to relate good news in others. Children can be encouraged to formulate messages in a way that takes into consideration their listener's feelings, e.g. tactfully, or in a way that 'saves face' in others, and how to avoid conveying bad news bluntly or without preparing the ground. They can also be encouraged to produce empathic and affective statements to console a friend in distress.

Pretend interviewing

Initiating and maintaining a topic of conversation, turn-taking and conversational skills can be practised in a pretend interview task. Children can practise ways of controlling a conversation, asking questions, eliciting responses, taking turns, producing open-ended questions, requesting clarification and providing adequate elaboration on their accounts. Pretend interviewing can take place in a pair or group setting where all children involved have the opportunity to contribute. Many themes relevant to the curriculum, such as historical themes, can be explored during this task, making the important link between classroom strategies that support language and the teaching and learning of specific subject matter.

Dilemma

In a dilemma situation, children learn how to use language to mediate social exchanges and resolve potential conflict. In their efforts to generate a solution and resolve a conflict, children must bring together a variety of language skills and social knowledge. Specifically, they should be able to use language effectively to exchange information, understand the feelings and points of view of the participants/listeners and offer and evaluate strategies to resolve the conflict. You may pose a dilemma by presenting a conflict situation and asking the children involved to agree or disagree with their classmate's opinion. In this context you may encourage them to negate another's argument, take a dominant role in a conversational exchange and influence others' thoughts and feelings and make persuasive appeals for the purpose of changing others' opinions and/or plans of action. Children who present communication difficulties tend to respond to others passively, or with minimum attempts to introduce and insist on their ideas and assume a more dominant role. A dilemma task can be easily introduced in the curricular context of religious/pastoral education, for example, where morally ambivalent issues are discussed.

Telling stories

Storytelling, in small groups or during circle time, is an effective method to support the development of language and communication skills in that it models purposeful conversations. During storytelling, language is used for the purpose of communicating ideas and experiences to others. Stories provide the basis for conversation, reasoning, stimulation of the imagination, all enhancing the understanding of implicit and explicit meanings. Storytelling is an excellent method that can be used with children of a wide range of ages, especially young children.

As discussed in Chapter 1, within the family context, young children use language mainly in a way that is supported by face-to-face interactions, gestures and body language. In the classroom, however, they are expected to share stories and talk about events and situations that are not experienced by the rest of the group. The demands to use language in a somewhat abstract manner can be too high for some young children who are not prepared or have limited practice with this type of conversation. There are ways to support them to develop the necessary language skills by helping them to

♦ predict the consequences of using particular linguistic forms (words, phrases, sentences)

♦ judge sentences as appropriate for a specific listener or setting. For example, discuss emotion words that can be said to a peer who is upset

♦ understand figurative language. For example, you can use metaphorical sentences and compare them to sentences that have explicit meanings

♦ understand correct word order via the knowledge of syntactic and grammatical rules

♦ reflect on the meaning of a sentence by providing the definitions of key words and phrases and engaging them in different interpretations, and

♦ construct riddles or use humour, and other forms of implicit language

For children who experience difficulties with story-telling it is helpful to provide them with story tapes and ask them to listen to them and re-create what they hear. You may also provide them with some key words to facilitate recall and the structuring of the story. As a start, you may give children story-books with pictures as a visual aid to assist them with the story recall. Another way of stimulating storytelling is by asking children to talk about their own experiences, e.g. a family trip or holidays, or events and situations that can relate to them personally. Overall, it is a good idea to encourage children to talk about their own interests and things that are meaningful to them. Partnerships with parents can support you in finding out about children's interests as well as the type of social interactions they encounter with family members and the surrounding community.

Circle time

These tasks, e.g. telling stories, referential task, dilemma, role-playing, can take place across curriculum structures. However, for young children, supporting their language and communication can be effectively done in the context of circle time. There is an increasing acceptance of the effectiveness of circle time in helping children develop language and communication skills to support learning and social adjustment. Circle-time interactions encourage the development and practice of the following skills:

♦ basic classroom skills (e.g. listening, concentrating, following instructions)

- communication skills (e.g. turn-taking, sensitivity to the listener's needs, providing background information, requesting clarification)

- friendship-making/sustaining skills, such as joining the group, initiating and maintaining conversation

- dealing with feelings in terms of understanding and using affect-denoting words, showing affection, recognizing others' emotions

- social problem-solving skills, such as resolving a conflict situation, dealing with emotionally charged situations, e.g. bullying, or presenting alternative solutions, and

- enhancing oral and written language by encouraging active participation in all areas of the curriculum

Circle-time activities can set the stage for you to provide a lot of encouragement and use language in ways that

- facilitate the flow of talking

- indicate active listening

- make positive comments

- elaborate on ideas expressed by the child, and

- help the child to achieve a clear purpose

(Raban and Ure 2000)

By involving children in the above-mentioned tasks, such as storytelling, pretend play, dilemma situations and circle-time activities, they can practise an array of language and communication skills including:

Making requests: for attention, objects, action, assistance, information and clarification. You can support children making requests by encouraging them to use gestures, e.g. hand-raising, pointing and eye contact, in the classroom to indicate what they know and what they do not, so that they can express their needs. By doing this, children learn that language can be used to express their own thinking/understanding and request more information or clarification, and at the same time, to influence others' thoughts and actions. It also helps them to become independent learners, responsible for monitoring their own understanding.

Turn-taking: you may explain to children the importance of turn-taking as well as discuss and demonstrate ways of achieving it. For example, you can practise with them how to use verbal and non-verbal means to obtain attention from the listeners when they want to contribute to a conversation, and also ways of understanding when the conversational topic shifts for them to respond accordingly. It is also important to stress that turn-taking behaviour varies across different social and cultural contexts (see Chapter 5 for a detailed discussion about the use of language in culturally diverse contexts).

Topic-management: this is a complex communicative skill in that it requires the ability to initiate a topic, maintain it for as long as it is required and change it when it is appropriate. It requires multiple language skills including adequate expressive and receptive vocabulary, understanding of non-verbal cues, being able to repair when a communicative breakdown occurs, providing clarification when necessary, taking into account listeners' needs and providing enough background information.

Being able to make requests, taking conversational turns and initiating and maintaining a conversational topic can also be fostered by employing structured activities that require a child to explain the steps taken and the outcomes expected. A few suggestions for activities by Gross (2002: 161) include:

♦ using computer software where one child creates and prints a picture and then has to give instructions to the partner at the keyboard so that they can re-create the image without the child showing the image

♦ using a box with materials (varying in colour, texture, shape) with one child choosing one and trying to describe it to the other child accurately enough so they understand what piece they are talking about

♦ having one child to tape-record instructions on how to make something and then having a group of children trying to follow the instructions

Supporting expressive and receptive language skills

Gross (2002) suggests a number of strategies to support the development of both receptive and expressive language skills with a particular emphasis on teaching skills required for making a request, engaging in problem-solving, greeting and initiating conversation, and for taking turns and being aware of the listener's need. The following suggestions to develop expressive and receptive language skills are based on Gross' teaching approaches to language development. To support children's expressive language, you may

♦ encourage them to ask questions for clarification, obtaining extra information, or eliciting others' ideas in a group

♦ develop a routine for children to greet each other, providing some key words and phrases for those with difficulties and encouraging them to repeat them

♦ facilitate the formulation of responses to others' questions in a group by providing some key words and phrases

♦ use the literacy hour to do some sentence-level work in terms of working on verbs, plural, possessives, prepositions (in, on, under, behind) and tenses

♦ encourage children, especially those with word-retrieval difficulties, to express themselves in any way they can, providing them with given alternatives, if necessary, and then asking them to elaborate on their answer

♦ model and encourage the use of 'What', 'When', 'How' and 'Why' questions

♦ expand vocabulary through the use of a dictionary, or visual maps in which children take a word and write other words that seem to relate to it to consolidate the learning of new words, and

♦ illustrate, through the use of riddles, word-games and jokes, that words can have many meanings

To support children's receptive language, you may

♦ get their attention by calling their name, or establishing eye contact before you address them

♦ refrain from speaking out of context and try to establish a background to the conversation

♦ place the child in a position so that he/she can pick up what is happening by watching other children

♦ use pictures and demonstrations

♦ break a long and complicated instruction or sentence into manageable components (task analysis)

♦ ask the child to repeat what you have just said

♦ use consistent vocabulary

♦ encourage children to use gesture or drawings to communicate an idea

♦ try to make time to offer several versions of what the child is trying to say

♦ use given alternatives, avoiding yes or no answers

♦ give children plenty of opportunity to talk about a shared experience, and

♦ speak slowly and clearly

ICT and language support

Developments in information and communication technology offer a range of opportunities to pupils by way of concept keyboards and overlays, speech synthesizers and touch screens, together with software such as computer-assisted writing programmes or integrated learning systems. Published research about the use and effectiveness of this equipment has mostly been small-scale, and there is no evidence that widely applied programmes such as integrated learning systems have a sustained effect or are necessarily any more effective than other instructional approaches. Where positive outcomes have been reported, the conditions of implementation were often particularly favourable (e.g. higher pupil–teacher and pupil–computer ratios, and a high level of teacher support and teacher–pupil interaction).

The *Code of Practice* (DfES 2001) clearly states that teachers should be supported in the use of ICT for pupils with special educational needs. ICT can be used for many purposes, i.e. writing individualized education plans (IEPs), keeping and managing pupils' records or, most importantly, assisting pupils with speech and language difficulties. With regard to the last, there are many technological devices which can be used to assist children's communication, especially children with speech difficulties. These include electronic language boards, voice-recognition software and voice synthesizers (Florian 2004). Also, the existence of networked communication helps children with speech and other communication difficulties to access a virtual world where they can communicate and build social networks and friendships. For example, Florian talked about virtual 'pen-pal' programmes through which pupils can email each other or visit 'buddies' websites (www.ebuddies.org) and communicate with other children.

The use of communication technologies can be very liberating for children with speech and language difficulties. However, there is some criticism with regard to the educational value that these technologies bring. In order to maximize the educational input, you need to plan carefully the educational activity and use communication technology as a tool, not a way of replacing good teaching. There is a widespread belief that unguided use of communication technology devices is unlikely to support learning. However, it is essential that you are supported by the school and other colleagues to develop the skills and confidence necessary to use new assistive technologies. An important contribution you can make is to maintain pupils' interest and motivation in the task and scaffold them by pointing to the relevant features of ICT. The latter promotes a teacher–pupil interaction, which in itself is crucial for encouraging language use.

Hegarty (2004) argues that teachers can contribute to a successful use of ICT by:

♦ encouraging interaction with pupils as well as between pupils

♦ identifying ICT tasks that can be useful by matching pupils' needs with task requirements

♦ scaffolding pupils by giving them prompts and then progressively reducing the prompts so they engage in the task independently

♦ presenting the use of assistive technology as a game or fun activity

For children who experience difficulties with written language, speech feedback on word-processors can be very helpful in improving the quality and accuracy of writing and motivate pupils to engage in editing when speech and spelling support is available. Built-in study and comprehension activities appear to facilitate learning from information texts, and imaginative presentation can be helpful – for example, phase-presentation can improve reading comprehension.

Summary

In this chapter, strategies to guide classroom practice with regard to supporting children with language and communication difficulties were discussed. It is accepted that no single approach works equally well with all pupils. Most children are likely to benefit from the strategies discussed in this chapter, especially as they are incorporated in the curriculum structure so they are not taught in an artificial and fragmented manner. It is essential that individual pupils' learning preferences, interests and style of communication are identified and used as the basis for an individual programme of language support.

4

Language and Social/Emotional Development

Language, social interactions and emotional maturity

[Communication skills are the cornerstone of effective interactions with peers and adults alike.] There is a growing body of research pointing to the importance of communication skills for developing and maintaining interpersonal relationships which in themselves are crucial for children's social adjustment and emotional maturity. A number of studies conducted by Prizant and his colleagues (1990; 1991) point to the interplay between language and social–emotional development in that children who are good communicators are capable of regulating behaviour and emotions in their interpersonal exchanges. This is particularly true for adolescents, whose friendships and peer interactions rely on conversations and the ability to use language to express subtle meanings, engage in empathic responses and relationship talk, give and receive advice and consolation, engage in self-disclosure and understand implicit messages and humour (see Gallagher 1993; Gottman 1983). In fact, conversational skills are so important for making friends that some language theorists and practitioners believe that it is even possible to predict children's friendships and social adjustment based on how they use language.

It is hard to think about the development of social skills in children in the absence of language. Gallagher argues that 'language is a primary means by which we make interpersonal contact, socialize our children and regulate our interactions' (1993: 11). Gottman has identified six sets of conversational skills that account for children's attempts to approach peers and make friends. Specifically, these include clarity of communication, connectedness and relevance to the topic, understanding of the listener's needs (perspective taking), disclosure of private thoughts, providing solutions to problems and expressions of empathy. Also, giving emotional support through the use of emotion words, initiating games, sharing jokes, explaining relationships between events and actions and reflecting on thoughts and emotions all enable children to relate to others meaningfully.

Making friends becomes central to children's social world, especially as they reach adolescence: a stage in which meaningful relationships and effective communication are highly valued. Having friends can be a significant source of empowerment and emotional support, whereas limited interpersonal experiences can be a major stressor for children and adolescents. Through friendships children create personal and social identities and construct social meanings that affect their behaviour and social adjustment. It is widely accepted that communication skills set the basis for dyadic interactions between friends. Friends use language to express empathy, provide social support messages (positive affective exchanges), negotiate and resolve conflict, reach consensus and generate social problem-solving strategies. These are subtle communication skills and acquiring them is not an easy undertaking, requiring opportunity, scaffolding/coaching and practice.

The revised *SEN Code of Practice* (DfES 2001) places an emphasis on the development of social and interpersonal skills, grouping them under the category of behavioural, emotional and social skills. Clearly, the development of social skills goes beyond managing behaviour to include language/communication, interpersonal relatedness and empathy.

Specifically, the *Code of Practice* states that pupils should be supported with:

♦ the development of social competence and emotional maturity

♦ adjusting to the school expectations and routines

♦ acquiring the skills of positive interaction with peers and adults

(DfES 2001: para. 7.60)

Language and social/emotional/behavioural difficulties: is there a link?

Donahue, Hartas and Cole (1998) argue that in recent years the interplay between language and social/emotional/behavioural difficulties in children has become increasingly evident. Along with that came the realization that language and social/emotional development are intertwined and thus they should not be approached separately when teachers and other practitioners work with children who present difficulties in these areas.

Language and Communication Difficulties

Teachers and parents are all aware that children with limited language and communication skills are likely to become frustrated in their interactions with others, frequently resulting in inappropriate behaviour, e.g. pushing, grabbing. Conversely, there is evidence (see McDonough 1989; Westby 1999) that children with behavioural/emotional difficulties tend to use immature language, with their vocabulary being very simplistic, finding it difficult to use abstract vocabulary and express multiple meanings, generate solutions to resolve conflict, take into consideration the listener's needs and produce empathic responses. It appears that children with emotional and behavioural difficulties present problems with the social use of language. For example, they are less skilled in initiating and maintaining a topic of conversation and providing appropriate responses to questions. They are also less likely to disclose information about themselves, which is the cement for interpersonal relationships, ask questions to elicit information from their conversational partners, make and maintain eye contact and contribute relevant information to a conversation.

We tend to group children who present difficulties with behaviour and social–emotional development into one homogeneous group. It is, however, important to make a distinction between internalizing and externalizing behaviour difficulties (Hartas 1996). Internalizing behaviour is understood as being directed towards (or targeting) the self and not others, and manifests itself as social withdrawal, avoidance, shyness, anxiety and even depression. In contrast, externalizing behaviour is manifested as aggression, anti-social behaviour and delinquency. It is certainly good practice to be aware of the differences in the communicative behaviour of these two groups of children and respond accordingly.

In every classroom, as you probably know, a lot of attention is given to children with behavioural difficulties in that they tend to be disruptive, prompting teachers to act decisively to manage their behaviour. In contrast, children who are shy or withdrawn do not receive much attention and support despite growing evidence that these children are likely to experience conversational difficulties. Evans (1987) examined the conversational skills of shy and withdrawn children during classroom conversations, role-playing tasks and free play, and found that these children's language is less mature, focusing primarily on 'here and now' activities and events. More specifically, children with internalizing behavioural difficulties tend to produce fewer and shorter sentences and their conversational topics lack variety and detail. They also present difficulties describing present and absent objects. During role-playing in particular, they tend to be less skilled in applying communication skills such as greeting, introducing the self or a conversational topic, comforting a peer and providing emotional support through the use of emotion words and empathic expressions. Also, during play, children who appeared withdrawn were found to make fewer requests for attention, fewer syntactically complex sentences, making instead more non-verbal requests, e.g. pointing, shaking head.

The reciprocal relationship between language/communication and social skills/behaviour management is instrumental especially for children with social/behavioural difficulties, as a large number of them are likely to present communication difficulties. Understanding the interplay between language and behaviour has important practical implications. Up until recently, providing language services to children with behavioural difficulties was not very common. There is, however, an increasing understanding that supporting behaviour through the development of language and communication skills holds immense potential.

Supporting behaviour and social/emotional adjustment via language

Teaching social skills is not an easy undertaking, partly because of their subjective nature, and partly because they involve many aspects, e.g. communication, understanding of social and cultural norms and practices, social motivation and value placed on social interactions. Clearly, good language and communication skills are central to the development of positive attitudes and social adjustment. It is logical to think that supporting conversational skills should be an important part of the remedial programmes for children with behavioural, social and emotional difficulties. However, traditionally, it has not always been the case.

In the light of the increasing evidence regarding the link between language, behaviour and emotional development, it is good practice to provide language support as a means of reducing inappropriate behaviour and enhancing social skills in the classroom and the playground. It is known that language develops when there are opportunities for interactions and the classroom structure allows for these to take place. One way of achieving this is to structure the classroom around collaborative, peer-mediated activities, e.g. collaborative learning, the 'buddy' system, as well as child-centred activities such as circle time and coaching. In the previous chapter I referred to circle time as an appropriate context to support the development of language and communication skills. Circle time has also the potential to be facilitative of children's social/ emotional development.

Circle time

Circle time is increasingly seen as an effective instructional method not only for helping children develop the communicative skills necessary for social interactions and active and independent learning but also to explore and understand their and others' emotional and social responses.

Mosley (1996) highlighted the contribution of circle-time activities to pupils with behavioural and emotional difficulties who are likely to display negative behaviours such as disruption and aggression, or withdrawal and depression. Such children are also likely to suffer from low self-esteem, lacking positive social models and having language/communication difficulties. Circle-time interactions are crucial for rebuilding their self-esteem by teaching them about empathy and ways of controlling themselves, and helping them achieve reasonable targets regarding behavioural standards in the classroom and the playground. Also, during circle time, children can learn how to use 'emotion' words to express their feelings and relate to other children meaningfully.

For young children in reception and early primary school classrooms, 'sharing experiences' during circle time can set the stage for talking about their personal experiences, giving them the opportunity to practise emotion words and narrative skills. You may ask them questions such as 'Who has a story to tell us?' to encourage them to narrate an event and out-of-school experience. For children with communication difficulties, adult support during this exercise is crucial. Sharing experiences has many benefits in that it allows children to talk about their lives, express their views and feelings, and this can be liberating especially in highly structured classrooms. During 'sharing experiences' time, it is important that you encourage pupils to produce more than just a short answer to your questions by helping them elaborate on their chosen topic. You should also encourage them to move freely from one activity or group to another to test their newly acquired linguistic skills and knowledge. This can be particularly beneficial for pupils who are shy and/or socially withdrawn in that they are given adequate opportunity to contribute to group discussions and to model appropriate interactions.

For older children, a literature-based approach is likely to contribute to the expansion of their vocabulary to include more complex/subtle emotion: words such as embarrassment, guilt or disappointment. You can choose a number of books containing stories with characters experiencing an array of complex emotions across diverse social situations. Direct discussions of the story characters' perspective and their interactions in a narrative context can support pupils' ability to take others' perspective and engage in 'emotion' speech. Stories can be a powerful tool for supporting language and social/emotional development, especially in pupils with behavioural/social and emotional difficulties and communication problems.

For children who are withdrawn or shy, you may

adopt certain strategies during circle time to enhance their self-esteem and, at the same time, support them conversationally. For example, by identifying their interests you are in a good position to set up social activities that allow expression of their interests.

A number of self-esteem strategies to boost children's self-esteem include:

◆ valuing all children's attempts, contributions and accomplishments

◆ avoiding interacting more with the more conversationally competent pupils

◆ making rules and standards of evaluation clear so students become evaluators of themselves

◆ avoiding comparisons and competition

◆ encouraging use of 'emotion' words to talk about their feelings

◆ supporting them to make positive statements about themselves by helping them to recognize what they are good at

◆ explaining to pupils with behavioural difficulties that it is not them that you do not approve of but their behaviour

◆ encouraging them to talk about commonly experienced events, e.g. a field-trip, computer activity, and last but not least

◆ providing children with low self-esteem with books that depict characters who express empathy towards others to teach both linguistic and social skills

(adapted from Woolfolk 1998 and Frederickson and Cline 2002)

Peer mediation

Another classroom technique that can be used in parallel with circle time is peer mediation. Peer-mediated interactions have been found to enhance interpersonal skills particularly in children with language and behavioural/emotional and social difficulties (see Audet and Tankersley 1999; Carriedo and Alonso-Tapia 1996).

Many American and Australian schools have successfully involved older pupils in mediation roles in the classroom and, most importantly, in the playground. A child who plays the role of a mediators should be capable of engaging in problem-solving and conflict-resolution. In order to become good mediators children should be supported to learn how to intervene by engaging in problem-solving. Also, it is important that they have a clear understanding of their role. For example, are they there to give advice and emotional support only, or do they actually have to generate solutions to a problem or just remind the others of a rule? Also, mediators are expected to scaffold the process of problem-solving by requesting background information regarding the conflict situation, generating strategies to resolve it, discussing the strategies with others and providing alternative ones when previous strategies fail.

Peer mediation sets the stage for modelling ways of using language effectively to influence others in a peaceful manner and ascertain leadership. Socially, peer mediation has been found to support the development and application of negotiation, communicative and problem-solving skills to resolve a conflict situation. Peer-mediated activities require good expressive/receptive language and social skills. For pupils to be part of the group and experience success, they need to be able to comprehend the vocabulary used, retain directions and rules in their short-term memory as they engage in an activity, formulate appropriate responses and understand the social dynamics of their interactions with others.

Peer-mediated strategies can be effective in increasing positive social and interpersonal interactions among children with behavioural difficulties, as well as supporting their communication skills. Developing peer/mentor support is an effective way of setting the stage for communicative and social interactions. In many US schools 'big brother/big sister' groups or 'buddies' have been implemented with success to support children who are less skilled socially and conversationally. These peer-support groups benefit all children involved, i.e. big brother/sister or 'leader'/'follower'. In this context, peers can help children with language and behavioural difficulties by modelling pro-social behaviour and providing direct language support through verbalizing negotiation strategies to resolve conflict or by just discussing a plan of action. You may supervise these peer-centred sessions and provide feedback and support if needed. You may also facilitate the process of problem-solving by asking pupils questions such as:

'What can we do to solve it?'
'Do you want some assistance?'
'How did you feel when . . . ?'
'What is the rule for . . . ?'

Peer-mediated activities can transform schools into more cooperative environments with reduced instances of bullying and other violations of children's rights. Pupils with behavioural and emotional difficulties are likely to benefit from peer mediation in terms of anger management, pro-social skills, development and empathy or taking into account others' feelings. Overall, peer-mediated interactions help pupils manage their behaviour and emotions by setting realistic demands, develop a clear and predictable structure of rewards and sanctions, value and respect the contribution of others, encourage both independent and collective work, support learning and build self-esteem, and ultimately create a less threatening environment for children to feel safe to explore different ways of learning.

Summary

Language and communication skills in children are crucial for successful social interactions and emotional maturity. There is growing evidence to support a link between language difficulties and social/emotional and behavioural difficulties. Understanding the interplay between language and behaviour has important implications in terms of classroom practice in that emotional and behavioural difficulties can be ameliorated via the development of language and communication skills. In this chapter, I referred to circle-time interactions and peer mediation as ways of supporting both behaviour and language in the classroom, to help pupils become emotionally mature and socially adjusted.

5

Language Difficulty or Language Difference?

Classroom language diversity

As global events create more refugees, economic migrants and asylum-seekers, British classrooms become increasingly multicultural and diverse. The number of children whose English is an Additional Language (EAL) is on the rise. Not all children learn an additional language in the same way. Some enjoy the learning process and are quite capable of making links between their own language and the newly acquired one. For other children it can be difficult because they experience either 'language needs' or 'special language needs' (Cline and Shamsi 2000). The differentiation between language needs and special language needs is paramount when determining assessment and provision for these children. 'Language needs' refers to the needs resulting from lack of proficiency in the additional language due to limited exposure and/or inadequate education. 'Special language needs' refers to difficulties that children experience not only with the additional language but, most importantly, with learning their first language. The latter suggests special educational needs (SEN) and requires special educational provision. In practice, this distinction is not always clear. Consequently, the confusion surrounding these terms has an impact on teachers' expectations of and understanding regarding children's language development, as well as the nature of classroom support.

Furthermore, the law about SEN states that

> a child is not to be taken as having a learning difficulty solely because the language (or form of the language) in which he is, or will be, taught is different from a language (or form of the language) which has at any time been spoken in his home.
>
> (Department for Education and Employment 1996, Section 312)

What this tells us is that children who come from linguistically diverse communities and who are at an early stage of learning English as a second language should not be labelled as having SEN. They are more likely to have language needs and not special language needs.

The *Curriculum Guidance for the Foundation Stage* (DfEE/QCA 2000: 19) recommends that teachers should support EAL children by

♦ building on their experiences of language at home and in the wider community by providing a range of opportunities to use their home language(s), so that their developing use of English and other language(s) support each other

♦ providing a range of opportunities for children to engage in speaking and listening activities in English with peers and adults

♦ ensuring that all children have opportunities to recognize and show respect for each child's home language

♦ providing bilingual support, in particular to extend vocabulary and support children's developing understanding

♦ providing a variety of writing in the child's home language as well as in English, including books, notices and labels, and

♦ providing opportunities for children to hear home language(s) as well as English, for example through the use of audio and video materials

The cultural context of language

The *Curriculum Guidance for the Foundation Stage* stresses the importance of taking into account children's home and community contexts. EAL children come to school from diverse family backgrounds, and bring with them not only another language but also a whole new set of experiences, beliefs and complex styles of interaction, having different rules for communication. These rules should not be disregarded, even if they do not fall into predictable patterns or familiar ways of interaction. With this in mind, collaboration with and negotiation between you and EAL children are crucial and can be achieved by offering them opportunities to reconsider, re-evaluate and reformulate meanings during their conversations.

I would like to illustrate the differences in the conversational styles in children from different cultures by discussing a specific example, i.e. storytelling/stories about personal experiences. Some children may tell a story by stating events, situations and characters in an implicit manner, whereas others may focus on one specific aspect/event of the story and go into more depth. Or, depending on the interactional styles and customs of their culture, they may have different ideas as to what parts of the story are relevant, when it is appropriate to take their turn (they may expect to see certain signals to indicate when it is OK to talk) or different approaches with regard to presenting a personal story to the public. Some children may feel uncomfortable sharing a personal story in front of a group, being more comfortable in a one-to-one conversation, whereas others may enjoy this performance.

With regard to language learning and other literacy skills, in some families children are exposed to pre-literacy behaviours and interactions from early on. Specifically, they are encouraged to share and discuss books with parents, write their own messages, have access to print and other educational resources, and receive answers to their questions in a meaningful communicative context. Families from different cultures have different approaches to the display of pre-literacy behaviours. For example, in certain cultures with a strong oral tradition, children are more involved in storytelling than formal reading or writing tasks. In others, especially rural communities, children may develop a more hands-on approach to learning, e.g. living on a farm and learning how to raise chickens or how milk is produced.

EAL classroom support

Almost half a century ago, Dewey (1956: 75) wrote:

> From the standpoint of the child, the great waste in school comes from his inability to utilise the experiences he gets outside of school in a complete and free way; while, on the other hand, he is unable to apply in daily life what he is learning at school.

This description is particularly relevant and timely for EAL pupils who are likely to experience a gap between home and school cultures, language and ways of social interaction. EAL pupils are more likely to experience the classroom culture and norms as being alien and not relevant to their own life, compared to pupils for whom English is their first language.

With Dewey's statement in mind, the learning activities that you plan to offer to EAL pupils need to be centred on their life experiences. You can facilitate their interactions and guide them to consider their peers as a source of help and support in their activities. By doing this, you give EAL pupils many opportunities to take conversational turns, offering and listening to each others' ideas and becoming conversational partners. In this context, language develops naturally.

Wells (1986) provides four recommendations for teachers to support pupils. These are relevant to and beneficial for EAL pupils.

♦ Assume that children engage in a conversation because they have something important to say. Their communicative attempts should be taken very seriously, even if they are incomplete or the language used is not accurate.

♦ Before responding, try to listen carefully to children's accounts and question your own understandings and biases about their culture. Ask children for clarification if necessary; by doing this, you send the message that they should also take responsibility during their conversations with others.

♦ When responding, address their point of view and extend their accounts by encouraging them to do the same.

♦ Be flexible in terms of calibrating your contributions. It is pedagogically appropriate for your contributions to be at, or slightly above, children's understanding. However, you need to be ready and able to modify your contribution in the light of the feedback that you receive from the pupils.

It is important that you keep these principles in mind when interacting with all pupils, particularly with those who come from diverse linguistic and cultural backgrounds. As Pappas, Kiefer and Levstik (1995) argue, language is a tool to communicate meaning via various linguistic patterns and styles. Children's activities and projects are surrounded by conversation. Thus, language cannot be understood, interpreted or evaluated unless it is related to the social contexts within which it is developed and used. In this way, language can be supported in a holistic way, avoiding isolated drills and practices on sub-systems of language, e.g. phonics, with no connection to other linguistic components, e.g. grammar, or semantics. Children from different linguistic and cultural backgrounds would then be supported to participate in the classroom discussion successfully, by ensuring that they are not involved in fragmented, separate activities for listening, speaking, reading or writing.

Currently in schools, there is an expectation that children should develop competence in standard English. The acquisition of standard English is an important goal of the National Curriculum, which states that

> in order for children to participate confidently in public, cultural and working life, pupils need to be able to speak, write and read standard English fluently and accurately. All pupils are therefore entitled to the full range of opportunities necessary to enable them to develop competence in standard English.
>
> (Department for Education 1995: 2).

This goal, i.e. meeting the language needs of children with EAL, is hoped to be achieved during the literacy hour. The National Literacy Strategy framework places an emphasis on listening and speaking through access to clear models of spoken standard English, and engagement in whole-class and group work, all within the clear structure of the literacy hour. Specifically, the National Association for Language Development in the Curriculum (NALDIC) Working Group (1998) suggested the following guidelines:

♦ take into consideration children's linguistic and social/cultural experiences located within their family and the community

- emphasize the importance of listening time, and provide some 'quiet time' for beginners

- support good peer models for oral language (perhaps create a 'buddy' system by pairing EAL children with more linguistically competent peers

- provide positive reinforcement and coaching of the target language (this can be beneficial not only for the EAL child but also for those who present language and communication difficulties)

- emphasize communication rather than correcting linguistic mistakes, in order to support self-confidence and maximize motivation to practise new skills, and

- create opportunities for using the target language across different contexts

Supporting EAL pupils' acquisition of standard English in the classroom is a balancing act: on the one hand, you need to take into consideration their social/ cultural context and their linguistic background and, on the other hand, you ask them to embrace a standard language that in most cases is practised in the context of school only. There is an ongoing debate on the pros and cons of encouraging EAL pupils to learn standard English. Adding to the controversy, there is a lack of appropriate assessment devices to assess EAL children's language needs and decide whether their difficulties are due to limited exposure to standard English or to underlying problems with language learning, also evident in their first language.

The Code of Practice for SEN Assessment (2001: para. 5.16) states that

Language Difficulty or Language Difference?

At an early stage a full assessment should be made of the exposure they have had in the past to each of the languages they speak, the use they make of them currently and their proficiency in them. The information about their language skills obtained in this way will form the basis of all future work with them both in assessing their learning difficulties and in planning any additional language support that is needed.

In practice, using standardized language tests to assess the language needs in non-English speakers may be invalid for several reasons. First, there are very few assessment tools standardized in languages other than English to be used with bi- or multilingual speakers. Secondly, standardized tests for the English language tend to favour monolingual speakers, in that those who speak a dialect and not standard English are likely to be disadvantaged. Thirdly, a standardized assessment is normally carried out in an artificial context, i.e. child–adult interaction in an assessment room, and not in the context of naturally occurring social interactions (e.g. family, classroom, playground).

For these reasons, it is important to take a qualitative approach to assessing the language needs of EAL pupils through discussions with the child's parents and other individuals from his/her community. This may not be feasible all of the time, in that some parents are not easily reached, perhaps due to their limited facility with English. In the latter case, employing an interpreter can help you to liaise with EAL pupils' families effectively. This interaction is important for you to gain information such as the degree of the child's exposure to languages in settings other than the classroom, i.e.

family, community, religious sites; the number of languages that are spoken at home and by the child's immediate family; the extent to which these languages are similar or different to English (linguistic distance between languages); the length of time the child has been living in the UK or other English-speaking countries; and, most importantly, whether the child experiences difficulties with the learning of his/her first language.

Classroom strategies

Integrated language: thematic units

Creating an integrated language classroom is the best way to give ample opportunities to EAL pupils to use language for many meaningful purposes. In an integrated language classroom, speaking, listening, reading and writing are not treated as separate subjects or activities but as tools that are used together for learning. An integrated language classroom can be achieved by taking a thematic unit approach. Through the use of thematic units, pupils learn not only the content or subject matter but also language *per se*, and this can be used across the curriculum. Indeed, the use of thematic units cuts across curriculum in that it integrates knowledge of subject matter, language, reading and writing. It also sets the stage for teacher–pupil collaboration, in that you pose questions for the pupils to think about, support their hypotheses and linguistic attempts and facilitate their choices.

The following is an example of a thematic unit to illustrate ways in which language can be used in the classroom to support learning. This thematic unit can be used with older children. Its title is 'Thinking about the Past' and its aim is to integrate language (speaking, listening), reading and writing.

> Within a collaborative group setting, pupils are encouraged to read and discuss books about historical fiction as well as history books and to consider a number of questions, such as 'How have various authors understood and thought about the past?', 'What evidence do they use?' 'How do they test the validity of the evidence, and does it matter to test it?', 'Do you agree with their point of view and why?', 'Do you see any similarities or common patterns between historical and current events?', 'Can you think of examples from current affairs/events/situations that have their roots in the past?' or 'Do you feel that you can relate to these historical events, and in what ways?'

Access strategies

Children with EAL can benefit from what Gross (2002) refers to as 'access or bypass strategies', as long as they experience language needs and not special language needs. Access strategies can be implemented in the mainstream with children working at the same level as their peers. In this context, the learning objectives are the same and the teaching style does not change. The access strategies aim at removing obstacles to learning posed by not having reached adequate proficiency with English as a second language.

The following is a list of access strategies based on a framework for practical guidance by Gross (2002) to

Language and Communication Difficulties

support children who speak English as an Additional Language:

♦ Simplify verbal instructions by using simple vocabulary and sentence structures, and by breaking long, multi-step instructions into simple manageable pieces.

♦ Use demonstration techniques after giving verbal explanations about how to do something. Use concrete examples, especially during arithmetic where key words have to be understood before a pupil does the mathematical operations.

♦ Use visual aids such as cards that link words with pictures.

♦ Avoid placing EAL pupils close to distractions and background noise to enable them to listen to you. Children who are learning to speak English have to concentrate hard to listen to individual sounds and make sense of what it is said. Also, you may call the pupil's name first before you direct a question to him/her.

♦ Avoid using language in an abstract manner by drawing links between the presented materials and examples from pupils' everyday life. Understanding abstract concepts can be particularly challenging for pupils whose linguistic capacity is at the early stages of development.

♦ Clarify and explain important vocabulary before engaging pupils in reading to facilitate comprehension. You may also create a glossary with the most frequently occurring words.

Language Difficulty or Language Difference?

♦ Simplify sentence structure during writing. For example, use short sentences, active and not passive verbs and not many grammatical features.

♦ Supplement books with tapes so pupils have the opportunity to listen to a text as well as read it. This facilitates listening comprehension, which is a crucial skill for EAL pupils.

♦ Encourage pupils to use alternatives to written presentations: pictures, drawings, key words, diagrams, or flowcharts.

♦ Provide prompt sheets for writing to ensure that there is a degree of structure to facilitate writing. Specifically, use cloze procedures, that is leaving sentences incomplete and giving the option of a number of words (e.g. verbs, nouns, adjectives, adverbs) so pupils can enter the correct one. Also, provide children with sentences or paragraphs to be put in the right order, and paragraph openings.

♦ Form reading groups and pair EAL pupils with other pupils who are competent readers. After having read the text ask them to talk about it. (I refer to this strategy as 'extended text' and discuss it in detail in Chapter 6.)

These strategies are inclusive in that they support learning in pupils who may not present difficulties with English *per se*, but who may experience concentration difficulties, dyslexia or any other SEN. Being access strategies, they do not target any area of SEN in particular. However, if the child presents special language needs in terms of displaying difficulties with the process of learning English, as well as his/her mother language, then access strategies may not be sufficient, in that, according to Torgesen (1996), SEN children require support that is targeted, structured, intensive and cumulative. This type of support can be provided through differentiation (a detailed description of differentiation strategies for children with language difficulties is given in Chapter 3).

Differentiation

The access strategies are effective for EAL pupils who have had a degree of exposure to English. There is a growing number of pupils, however, who find themselves in British classrooms having had very limited exposure to English, if any at all, as a result of unforeseen changes in their life, e.g. refugee children or children of asylum-seekers. For this group of EAL pupils differentiation may be deemed to be necessary. You are likely to face numerous challenges teaching this group in that they are at a very early stage in their English-based schooling. Thus it is not clear as to whether they display language needs or special language needs (e.g. specific language impairment or dyslexia, or both). Also, you are less likely to obtain information about their language development from their parents or carers in that they themselves are likely to have difficulties communicating in English and/or liaising with schools effectively. Moreover, there are limited assessment tools that can be used with non-English-speaking children to obtain valid results regarding their first-language development in terms of delineating their linguistic profile and needs. This is a grey area, and you are left with very limited information about these children's language development, first or additional language(s), and their educational background.

The literacy hour provides an effective structure for differentiation. During the literacy hour, EAL children are encouraged and helped to engage in activities such as sequencing letters and words, sorting words according to the initial sound, listening to a tape, attempting word recognition or putting words in order to make sentences. As I will discuss in detail in the next chapter, language and reading go hand in hand, with some theorists in the field of reading going so far as to suggest that reading is 'speech written down'. Thus it is not only that language development supports reading but also the other way around in terms of reading supporting language. With this in mind, reading (both with differentiated and non-differentiated instruction) can help EAL pupils with the acquisition of English in terms of developing their vocabulary, their knowledge of sentence structure (grammar and syntax) and an understanding of the meaning of words. Ann Browne (2003) argues that EAL pupils do not necessarily have to wait to develop good oral language skills before they start learning to read. In fact, Gregory (1996) ascertains that children can read before they reach a degree of proficiency in the new language, with reading leading to oral language development.

The following is an example of differentiation during reading that can take place in the context of the literacy hour for a child whose level of proficiency in English as a second language is very poor. To support EAL pupils with reading, you can prepare the ground by discussing the story/text and explaining the key words to the whole group. Then for the EAL pupils you may need to (a) set different learning objectives, e.g. read one instead of two paragraphs, or read a book with plenty of illustrations; (b) modify teaching practices by, for example, giving the children a set of simple 'wh' questions to guide their reading, using pictures as clues to facilitate comprehension, working on phonics to support them with word recognition; and (c) removing obstacles to learning by using videos or tapes to give them the opportunity to listen to books being read.

Setting different learning goals gives EAL pupils the opportunity to increase their awareness about the sounds of language through letter–sound correspondences. Some languages, e.g. Greek, Spanish, have what is called a 'transparent phonology', in that the patterns between sound and letters are predictable and consistent. Thus it is possible that EAL pupils whose first language is characterized by transparent phonology expect to find the same level of alphabetic and phonological consistency in English. In this case, they need to be introduced slowly to the phonological rules of the English language, requiring an adjustment of the learning goals with respect to raising phonological awareness and teaching phonetic rules.

Modifying your teaching approach is particularly important for EAL pupils. You may encourage the development of speaking and listening skills by asking pupils to repeat instructions, expanding their contributions, selecting reading materials whose content is relevant to their lives, and giving them time to think and formulate their answers. Giving them extra time is important, in that it takes EAL pupils longer to locate appropriate vocabulary, apply syntactic and grammatic rules and formulate sentences.

Language Difficulty or Language Difference?

Some EAL pupils speak languages other than English at home, so it is crucial for them to get as much exposure to English as possible during the school day if we are to help them acquire it as a second language. In the context of teaching modification, EAL pupils are likely to benefit from specialized, language-based instruction for reading and writing. Language support strategies may include:

♦ Previewing all reading materials to establish background knowledge prior to reading. You can do this by talking about the key ideas of the text and drawing links between these ideas and children's interests and existing knowledge.

♦ Utilizing prefixes and suffixes to illustrate changes in meaning and enhance children's vocabulary development. This can make them aware of the connection between certain linguistic elements (e.g. -s- for plural, -ed- for past tense) and meaning.

♦ Enhancing sound-blending skills and presenting new words linguistically; focus on root words, prefixes and suffixes. By doing this, you emphasize the role of phonology, a language component, in supporting reading.

♦ Emphasizing contextual word decoding by providing picture cues or reminding pupils of the main idea, simultaneously drawing their attention to initial letters to narrow down the word choices.

♦ Encouraging acquisition of sight-word vocabulary by placing new words on cards and reviewing them daily to encourage pupils' proficiency.

Language and Communication Difficulties

Removing obstacles to reading and language for EAL pupils also involves a degree of understanding on your part about the Western cultural contexts and references made in texts. Meaning-making during reading relies heavily on our familiarity with the beliefs, attitudes, societal and cultural knowledge expressed in the text in hand. We make assumptions that are culture-specific, and we tend to take them for granted without realizing the difficulties that a non-British reader may experience in trying to make sense of an unfamiliar text. It is important to choose books from the children's point of view to ensure that they can relate to content and cultural references. One way of achieving this is by finding out about EAL pupils' experiences and interests. It is important to recognize and value their knowledge of other languages and use that knowledge to support the learning of English.

You can also remove obstacles for EAL pupils who are likely to experience difficulties with listening comprehension by implementing a number of strategies to facilitate the presentation of instructions, including:

◆ maintaining eye contact during verbal instruction

◆ making directions clear and concise and being consistent with daily instructions

◆ simplifying complex directions and avoiding multiple commands

◆ ensuring that children understand the instruction before they begin the task

◆ repeating instructions in a calm, positive manner if necessary

◆ making children feel comfortable when seeking assistance, and

◆ reducing stress, pressure and fatigue that can break down children's self-control and motivation

With regard to the last point, there is research evidence to suggest that children in the early stages of learning a new language experience fatigue and stress that themselves present further obstacles in accessing the curriculum.

Summary

Children from diverse linguistic and social/cultural backgrounds bring into the classroom different languages as well as different styles of interaction, values and attitudes towards learning. You, as a teacher, have a daunting, albeit rewarding, task to support pupils who learn English as a second language, in that it is not always clear whether they experience language needs or special language needs. Taking an integrated approach to teaching language in the classroom through the use of thematic units, you can help them realize that speaking, listening, reading and writing are not separate subjects or activities but tools that can be used together for learning English. Finally, it is hoped that the use of access strategies as well as differentiation (setting different learning goals, modifying teaching and removing obstacles) will help you to deal successfully with this grey area of language needs.

6

Language, Curriculum Access and Academic Performance

The role of language in children's learning

Language is used to represent, analyse and communicate knowledge and information. Through language, children organize, discuss and present knowledge to the outside world and, ultimately, learn. The social role of language manifests itself in our ability to establish membership with social and cultural groups, share information with others and participate in social exchanges, e.g. storytelling, dialogue, classroom discussions. Finally, language has an expressive function in terms of articulating feelings, beliefs and attitudes and developing a sense of personal identity. Within the classroom, there is the 'pupil' language, the 'teacher' language and the language of the curriculum and the subject matter. The dialogue between pupils and teachers is expected to clarify, expand and make links between new and prior knowledge, and ultimately help pupils learn.

As language develops, children learn not only the structure of the language but also how to use it for numerous communicative purposes. The medium of classroom interaction is conversation, an important means by which pupils express the meaning of their experiences, intentions and ideas. A fundamental question for every teacher to ask is: 'What is the general nature of conversation and how is it organized in the classroom?'

These multiple functions and facets of language are reflected in the National Curriculum guidelines in that, according to them, children at Key Stage 1 and 2 are expected to be able to

♦ speak for different audiences

♦ listen and respond, and

♦ engage in discussion and group interaction

Breaking these skills into specific tasks, it becomes apparent how central language is to children's learning and social development. Listening, responding and using language as a learning and social tool to support social interactions and academic performance involve the ability to

♦ understand and ask questions

♦ answer a simple direct question by talking about (a) a personal experience, (b) a story, or (c) subject-specific knowledge

♦ use grammar and syntax properly

♦ ask peers simple questions to initiate contact, or obtain information

♦ engage in peer collaborative work (e.g. talk about text)

♦ ask questions for clarification or to obtain information

- participate in role-playing activities

- use questions to obtain information about abstract events or hypotheses

- respond to others' questions during an activity or homework

- respond to a question and justify a point of view

- participate actively in classroom discussions

- follow instructions, and

- apply social problem-solving skills when necessary

It is widely accepted that language is fundamental to the development of both literacy and numeracy skills. A large number of studies have established a link between language and reading in particular. In this chapter, I will focus on the interplay between language and reading, given that reading cuts across all areas of the curriculum, and discuss ways in which language supports reading development, and vice versa.

Although language and reading develop separately, in that language develops naturally and reading through teaching and practice, their pathways cross and become intertwined from the very early stages of children's learning. Many researchers in the area of literacy (e.g. Catts and Hugh 1996; Kamhi and Catts 1989) have looked at the relationship between language and reading and pointed out that reading involves both spoken and written language. Children learn to read by integrating linguistic meaning and form verbally and visually. Specifically, recognizing words requires a good knowledge of the phonological aspect of language (sounds), whereas extracting meaning from text relies on good semantic (meaning) and syntactic knowledge, as well as an awareness of the social/cultural context within which the text is located. Thus, during reading, children actively integrate diverse pieces of linguistic and social knowledge in order to extract meaning from text.

Evidence regarding the close relationship between language and reading comes mainly from intervention programmes, where the emphasis is on the development of spoken language skills as a means of supporting reading accuracy and reading comprehension. Therefore, it is logical to argue that children with language difficulties, e.g. problems with word-finding, use of immature grammatical structures, lack of organization and problems with sequencing, are also likely to present difficulties with reading.

Phonology and reading: figuring out the sounds of language

One language ability in particular that has been found to underlie reading is phonology, that is an awareness of or sensitivity to the speech sounds of language (e.g. Elbro et al. 1998; Gillon and Dodd 1994). An impressive amount of research indicates that phonological sensitivity and early phoneme analysis are very strong predictors of later reading development in children (Goswami 1995; Torgesen, Wagner and Rashotte 1994). Reading and phonology begin to interact with each other at the word-recognition stage where, in order to decipher and sound out words, children need to make links between the letters they see in print and the sounds they hear.

Once they have read/recognized the printed words, children are ready to engage in the process of extracting meaning and drawing links with prior knowledge.

Before discussing phonology and its links with reading, I would like to explain some of the terms used when referring to phonological processing and phonological skills development in children. Several terms, including phonological awareness, phonological sensitivity and phoneme analysis/decoding or recoding, are used interchangeably. However, it is important to delineate their meaning and map their links to reading. Phonological awareness refers to an explicit knowledge of the sounds that comprise words. We use different sounds to distinguish words with distinct meanings, and these sounds are known as the phonemes of the language (a phoneme is the smallest unit of sound). The term 'phonological awareness' refers to our ability to recognize sounds and sound patterns in spoken language. Once we recognize them, we are able to manipulate and understand the sound structure of words. Also, there is a need to draw a distinction between syllabic awareness and phonological awareness, in that the latter is thought to proceed from an awareness of syllables to an awareness of phonemes.

According to Oakhill and Garnham (1989), phonological awareness is a general term used to describe the ability to detect, distinguish and manipulate the sounds of words such as syllables, onset rimes and phonemes. Awareness of large sound units (e.g. rhyme) develops in the majority of children without any problems. A higher level of phonological awareness, also known as phonetic awareness, involves an awareness of smaller sound units, i.e. phonemes. Children need to develop a good knowledge of the alphabet and the letter–sound correspondences in order to attain this level of phonological processing. Phonological sensitivity refers to the recognition of the phonological aspects of the spoken language such as rhyme and alliteration.

Knowledge of sound–letter correspondences and phoneme discrimination is a crucial first step towards reading development. Phonological competence, or the ability to use systematic relationships between letters and phonemes, can be assessed by asking children to read novel strings of letters (nonwords) or to tell which nonwords sound like real words. For example, you may give children a list containing words that are not real, such as 'vasp', and 'poth', and ask them to sound them out and also find out the real words that sound like these nonwords. In this example, 'vasp' sounds like 'clasp' and 'poth' like 'moth'. It is thought that children who cannot read nonwords correctly are likely to experience reading difficulties, manifested in terms of deciphering and recognizing unknown words in particular (i.e. word-recognition, word-attack skills).

The most widely accepted explanation for reading difficulties is inability to process the phonological features of language in terms of analysing/synthesizing sounds and linking them to letters. This is normally assessed by tasks such as the above (e.g. nonwords) and also by asking children to name a sequence of familiar pictures depicting numbers, letters, colours or objects at speed. Difficulties with these tasks normally become apparent at the early stages of schooling, e.g. nursery, and are currently viewed as the core problem underlying reading difficulties, including dyslexia.

Making meaning through conversations: extending the text

Because language consists not only of sounds but also sentences and conversations, children need to be able to recognize individual words, and also use background knowledge about language to draw analogies and make inferences to facilitate reading comprehension. As phonological knowledge is important for word recognition, the syntactic and grammatical knowledge of language is equally critical for reading comprehension in that readers use a variety of syntactic and grammatical cues to comprehend text. Children's reading progresses by acquiring a sequence of complex linguistic skills. For example, after reaching a level where pupils are able to use sound–letter correspondence rules (phonetic rules), grammar and syntactic rules that require knowledge of the word structure normally follow without any problems. Children have to develop all these skills, i.e. phonological, syntactic, grammatical, in order to be able to pronounce words. For example, assuming that children develop syntactic knowledge only, then they will be less able to pronounce words correctly. To illustrate this, '-ed' is pronounced differently in different contexts, e.g. as in 'liked' and 'located', although the syntactic information remains the same (Martlew 1992).

An interesting way of bridging conversational skills and reading is through talking about the text. This is known as extending the text through the use of language, suggesting that language is involved in the process of making and sharing meaning. Talking about books can take place at any point during reading, at the beginning, middle or end. Before even opening the book, just by looking at its cover, children can start talking and speculating about its content. When working with children with language and communication difficulties, you may need to scaffold a dialogue around the text by contributing and/or responding to their comments. During reading, children are able to engage with a book at many levels. One level involves an immediate reaction to the pictures in the book. For example, children may say, 'Oh my daddy has a car like this', after seeing the picture of a car in a book or on its cover. Another level may involve commentary about the characters or the main activity/event. Here, they have the opportunity to use language to explore/infer other people's thoughts and feelings. At this stage of reading, you also have the opportunity to extend children's vocabulary by introducing new words and incorporating them in the conversation. You can stimulate the conversation through open-ended but focused questions, encouraging children to use complex language to build elaborate language structures. You can also help them realize that, through listening and speaking, we build on the ideas of others and achieve rich interpretations of the texts we read.

The contribution of language towards understanding text is manifested during children's collaborative reading activities where they are encouraged to talk about what they read and construct meaning through talking. Talking about the text seems to extend it, in that children have the opportunity to express ideas, make comments and ask questions to enhance their reading comprehension. Also, teacher-guided discussions of literature and teacher–pupil conversational interactions are likely to facilitate pupils' understandings of the main themes or ideas expressed in the text.

Harker argues that story discussions expand the boundaries of reading by focusing not only on the text being read but also on the conversation or 'extended text' that is socially constructed during group talk as pupils interact with one another and the text (Harker 1988). Story discussions also encourage a dynamic approach towards meaning-making by taking others' points of view and interpreting their thoughts, clarifying expectations and negotiating the purpose of reading and, ultimately, monitoring their own understanding. In the USA, the Book Club program (Raphael and McMahon 1994), for example, encourages children to support their reading comprehension through conversations and suggests ways of talking about the text. This programme appears to support reading by integrating language and literacy goals within the context of collaborative classroom interactions (i.e. whole-class discussions, pupil-led group discussions).

Children with language and reading difficulties

There is evidence to suggest that speech and language delays at the age of 5 will most certainly affect reading and, even where difficulties are resolved in early school years, school-age children may continue to need support. Pupils with language and reading difficulties benefit from an explicit focus on teaching phoneme-awareness, segmentation and blending, reading materials at their language comprehension level, participating in paired and shared reading and from a structured, whole-class literacy instruction combined with individual instruction for both reading and language.

The National Association for Special Educational Needs (NASEN) has published a useful guide on identifying reading difficulties at a word level and a sentence level. At a word level, phonological difficulties hinder children's understanding about how sounds and letters relate to each other, resulting in problems in deciphering unknown words. At a sentence-level, because of grammatical and syntactical difficulties and a restricted knowledge of semantics (word meaning), children are not able to integrate the information they get and extract meaning. This is possible even when they are able to recognize individual words. Clearly, language is heavily implicated in reading at both word and sentence level. At a word level, pupils need to apply phonetic rules accurately and consistently to decipher words; otherwise their chances of pronouncing words correctly are limited. At a sentence level, when vocabulary is difficult and the sentences are complex in terms of grammar and syntax, children with language difficulties are less equipped to make connections between words, draw links with what they already know and extract meaning.

Classroom strategies for reading and language

The application of the general principles of good classroom practice (e.g. time on task, guided practice, relevant feedback) is as important as taking specific instructional approaches to focus on elements of literacy, such as paired reading. With regard to paired reading, studies show that both parents and peers can be effective if trained. Equally important is your ability, as a teacher, to assess children's reading comprehension by skilled questioning, so that their attention is directed to meaning-making as well as the mechanics of word-decoding.

Effective learning strategies for pupils with language and reading difficulties are characterized by being structured, sequential, cumulative and thorough (Torgesen 1996). These children also benefit from phonetics teaching (though onset-rime awareness precedes phonemic segmentation), overlearning and a multisensory approach, all of which help them to make links between sound, symbol and written form.

Given that language and reading interact with each other, you may combine language and reading goals and apply classroom strategies that target both. Specifically, certain language-based strategies advocated by DfES to support reading include:

♦ demonstrating phonological processing (linking phoneme and letter – grapheme): using games to show pupils, especially in early years, how sounds and letters connect

♦ modelling reading comprehension by setting up shared reading activities where children converse about text, e.g. make comments and exchange ideas

♦ scaffolding pupils by assisting them with reading, for example asking questions to facilitate and/or extend their comprehension

- providing explanations to clarify unknown words and giving certain cues to support comprehension of text

- initiating and guiding exploration. This can take place during individual or group reading where conversation is used as tool for understanding the text

- investigating ideas. This is a way of going beyond the text by making inferences to ideas, connections with existing knowledge, drawing conclusions and predicting what is going to happen next

- discussing and helping pupils to engage in reasoned arguments

- listening and responding to pupils' contributions

The majority of these suggestions point to the fundamental role that language plays during reading. You may implement them by forming small reading groups and asking children to choose the book(s) they would like to read. First, ask them to speculate about the story content by looking at the title and illustrations. They may have come across a similar title or book before so they are encouraged to talk about what they already know about the theme, the author or the illustration. Secondly, encourage children to read the story and engage in discussion. You may also be part of the discussion that should be built around the ideas introduced by the pupils. At this stage you can also provide support and encouragement to the less vocal children in the group. Finally, you may encourage children to bring ideas together, draw conclusions and make predictions about future events/situations as a way of giving a closure to their reading.

Training on the language sounds (phonology)

The National Curriculum and the literacy hour place an emphasis on the teaching of phonological skills to support children's reading development (e.g. word-attack skills, word recognition, fluency). Children who present difficulties with the sounds of language can benefit from a phonological approach. Phonological knowledge is crucial to enable them to attack words successfully. When faced with an unfamiliar word, children who have acquired phonological knowledge are able to apply phonetic rules to break it down in order to read it. You may implement the following strategies to enhance children's phonology:

♦ encourage them to look for recognizable units such as syllables (un-, re-), and word-endings (-ing, -tion)

♦ teach them how to look for the pattern of vowels and consonants by marking them with 'v' or 'c', and then help them to decide how to break up the syllables

♦ read each syllable separately and ask them to repeat it

There are also many specialist programmes (e.g. Alpha to Omega) that focus on phonological training by analysing the sound structure of words. Their main goal is to help pupils develop an awareness about the links between letter and sound and how to manipulate them in order to sound them out and decipher words.

Cooke (2002) has compiled a list of behaviours and skills that are associated with the development of phonological skills. This list is a very useful tool to help

you identify pupils who are suspected of having difficulties with the sound system of language.

Specifically, you may check if a pupil

♦ can separate individual words in the flow of speech

♦ is aware of the sounds that comprise single words

♦ can identify words that rhyme

♦ knows how to blend the sounds of a word

♦ makes correspondences between single sounds
and letters

♦ can differentiate between vowels and consonants

♦ can build words consisting of consonants and vowels

♦ can decipher words that he/she has not seen before,
and

♦ can separate and blend sounds automatically during
reading

Following this list, you will be able to chart pupils'
phonological profile of strengths and weaknesses, and
apply appropriate strategies to teach phonics. Cooke
states that there is a specific order of teaching phonics
that you should follow, with a lot of revision built into
the process. It is important to start by focusing on the
links between letters and single sounds and simple
word structures, such as words comprised of consonant–vowel–consonant (cvc). What should come next is
the different consonant digraphs (i.e. 'sh', 'th', 'ch'), and
then the consonant blends. Some children have difficulties perceiving the individual sounds in consonant

blends, for example, /sh/, and thus they may pronounce the word 'ship' as 'sip'. Also, triple blends such as 'str' and 'shr' can be particularly challenging for some children to grasp, and so are short and long vowels (Cooke 2002).

Supporting reading comprehension

Language difficulties have a negative impact on the comprehension aspect of reading. It is crucial to ameliorate language difficulties before implementing reading comprehension strategies which themselves rely on a sound linguistic knowledge. Cooke (2002) refers to a number of reading strategies that are illustrative of the extent to which language skills underlie reading comprehension. Their aim is to alleviate reading difficulties via the language route. Specifically, during reading, you may consider:

♦ Using cloze exercises. Ask children to read incomplete sentences and fill in the gap by using a word chosen from several options. This task requires syntactic and grammatical skills and knowledge about word meanings and word associations. It is more difficult to fill in a noun or verb compared to grammatical features such as articles.

♦ Helping children understand the purpose of reading. This will also make them appreciate the complexity of the language used. For example, in narratives, the language involves the use of words that describe the characters' feelings, intentions and thoughts, details of the setting, etc. When we read the text to obtain information we tend to use language in a way that helps us summarize key points and synthesize details into coherent units. Finally, viewing the text as providing the context for discussion, the language becomes more demanding, in that a reader needs to form arguments that are relevant to the content of the text and which, at the same time, draw general themes and go beyond the boundaries of the book.

♦ Developing an awareness of the sounds of language and ways of separating and integrating them to decipher and pronounce unknown words.

♦ Developing self-monitoring strategies to make pupils aware of their own learning and capable of taking the initiative to ask questions or clarify things further. Retelling a story, for example, can help a pupil organize the information in a coherent way, getting the important facts when reading for information, making inferences (reading between the lines), making connections with existing knowledge, drawing conclusions, making predictions and, ultimately, adopting a critical approach.

You can certainly facilitate reading comprehension by making children aware of the stages involved in achieving it. The first stage of reading involves self-questioning, the second stage relies on exploration of the text individually or collectively through peer talk, and the third stage is the closure or wrapping up of reading which involves pupils' reflection on the text read and organization of the newly acquired information. The aim of self-questioning and peer talk during reading is twofold, in that they support the development of both reading and language/communication skills in an integrated manner.

Pupils in peer groups should be asked to read text silently, ask self-monitoring questions, engage in peer discussions, provide a summary of the paragraphs they read and answer factual and inferential questions. This procedure allows you to look at whether children use language appropriately, engage in reasoned argumentation, ask for clarification and provide adequate explanations. The following is a brief description of how self-questioning and peer talk, both language-based functions, can be incorporated during reading.

Self-questioning

Reading is assisted through the use of language as a thought-supporting mechanism ('think-aloud'). Specifically, pupils learn how to use certain strategies (e.g. plan, revise, cross-examine text information with background knowledge, monitor comprehension) that are known to support reading comprehension. These strategies can be implemented through peer talk and self-questioning. Regarding the latter, during reading, pupils may ask themselves questions such as:

♦ What is this paragraph mainly about?

♦ Is there anything that I am not sure about?

♦ How does it link with previous paragraphs?

♦ Does it make sense?

♦ What is likely to come next?

Peer talk

During small-group reading, you should encourage pupils to talk about what they have read with each other in the group. You may prompt them to start talking about the facts, make inferences based on the information they have, request clarification if they need to support an argument, make connections to background knowledge and finally draw conclusions. To this end, you may ask them a number of factual and inferential comprehension questions about:

♦ the main characters' feelings and thoughts (if it is a story)

♦ facts, events and situations

♦ definitions and explanations of general statements

♦ comparisons/contrasts by showing the similarities and differences between ideas

♦ groupings of ideas based on their shared features

♦ the linguistic structure of text (e.g. word meanings, grammar/syntax rules, use of figurative language – metaphors)

♦ causal relationships between ideas (e.g. cause and effect), and

♦ predictions about future events or situations

Towards the end of the reading session you may ask pupils to give a summary of what they read and also ask them to reflect about the ways they can link new information and ideas with what they already know.

Both self-questioning and peer talk should be monitored by you to ensure that all pupils in the group participate and benefit from it, especially children who present language and/or reading difficulties who may be less forthcoming in their verbal contributions. Self-questioning and peer talk facilitate reading for pupils with language and reading difficulties by encouraging pupils to talk and collectively explore and make meaning when reading books.

Summary

In this chapter I discussed various ways of supporting the development of reading skills in pupils via the language route. In the classroom, you can start by supporting pupils to acquire phonological skills, or an awareness of the language sounds, and gradually move towards demonstrating how language can be used to talk with their peers about text, ask questions and make meaning. Clearly, language is implicated in reading at word level (phonology), sentence level (grammar, syntax) and text level (meaning-making through discussion and self-questioning). Combining language and reading goals in the classroom brings together diverse aspects of the curriculum in an integrated manner.

References

Audet, L. and Tankersley, M. (1999) *Use of self-talk strategies to enhance comprehension and behaviour*, poster session presented at annual American Speech-Language-Hearing Association convention, Boston, MA.

Beveridge, M. and Conti-Ramsden, G. (1987) *Children with Language Disabilities*. Milton Keynes: Open University Press.

Browne, A. (2003) *A Practical Guide to Teaching Reading in the Early Years*. London: Paul Chapman.

Bruner, J. (1987) 'The transactional self', in J. Bruner and H. Haste (eds) *Making Sense: The Child's Construction of the World*. London: Methuen.

Carriedo, N. and Alonso-Tapia, J. (1996) 'Main idea comprehension: training teachers and effects on students', *Journal of Research in Reading* 19: 111–27.

Catts, H. W. and Hugh, W. (1996) 'Defining dyslexia as a developmental language disorder. An expanded view', *Topics in Language Disorders* 16 (2): 14–29.

Cazden, C. B. (1988) *Classroom Discourse: The Language of Teaching and Learning*. Portsmouth, NH: Heinemann.

Cline, A. and Shamsi, T. (2000) *Language Needs or Special Needs? The Assessment of Learning*

Difficulties in Literacy among Children Learning English as an Additional Language: A Literature Review. London: DfEE

Cooke, A. (2002) *Tackling Dyslexia* (2nd edn). London: Whurr.

Department for Education (DfE) (1994) *Code of Practice on the identification and assessment of Special Educational Needs.* London: HMSO.

Department for Education (DfE) (1995) *Key Stages 1 and 2 of the National Curriculum.* London: HMSO.

Department for Education and Employment (DfEE) (1996) *Education Act.* London: DfEE Publications.

Department for Education and Employment (DfEE) (1998) *The National Literacy Strategy Framework for Teaching.* London: DfEE.

Department for Education and Employment (DfEE) (1999) *The National Curriculum for England.* London: DfEE/QCA.

DfEE/QCA (2000) *Curriculum Guidance for the Foundation Stage.* London: QCA.

Department for Education and Skills (DfES) (2001), *Code of Practice on Identification and Assessment of Special Educational Needs.* London: HMSO.

Department for Education and Skills (DfES) (2001), *Special Education Needs Code of Practice.* London: DfES.

Dewey, J. (1956) *The Child and the Curriculum at the School and Society.* Chicago, IL: University of Chicago Press.

Donahue, M., Hartas, D. and Cole, D. (1998) 'Research on interactions among oral language and behavioural/emotional disorders', in D. Rogers-Adkinson and P. Griffith (eds) *Communication Disorders and*

Children with Psychiatric and Behavioural Disorders. San Diego, CA: Singular.

Elbro, C., Borstrom, I. and Petersen, D. (1998) 'Predicting dyslexia from kindergarten: the importance of distinctness of phonological representations of lexical items', *Reading Research Quarterly* 33: 36–57.

Evans, M. A. (1987) 'Discourse characteristics of reticent children', *Applied Psycholinguistics* 8: 171–84.

Florian, L. (2004) 'Uses of technology that support pupils with special educational needs', in L. Florian and S. Hegarty (eds) *ICT and Special Educational Needs. A Tool for Inclusion*. New York and Buckingham: McGraw-Hill/Open University Press, pp.7–20.

Frederickson, N., and Cline, T. (2002) *Special Educational Needs, Inclusion and Diversity. A Textbook*. Buckingham: Open University Press.

Gallagher, T. M. (1993) 'Language skills and the development of social competence in school-age children', *Language, Speech and Hearing Services at Schools* 24: 199–205.

Gillon, G, and Dodd, B. (1994) 'The effects of training phonological, semantic, and syntactic processing skills in spoken language on reading ability', *Reading and Writing* 6: 321–45.

Goswami, U. (1995) 'Phonological skills in learning to read', *Annals,* New York Academy of Sciences, 682: 296–310.

Gottman, J. (1983) 'How children become friends', *Monographs of the Society for Research in Child Development* 48: 1–86.

Gregory, E. (1996) *Making Sense of a New World*. London: Paul Chapman.

Gross, J. (2002) *Special Educational Needs in the Primary School: A Practical Guide* (3rd edn). Buckingham: Open University Press.

Harker, J. O. (1988) 'Contrasting the content of two story-reading lessons: A propositional analysis', in J. L. Green and J. O. Harker (eds), *Multiple Perspective Analyses of Classroom Discourse,* Vol. 28, *Advances in Discourse Processes*: Norwood, NJ: Ablex, pp. 49–70.

Hartas, D. (1996) 'Verbal interactions of children with internalising and externalising behaviour disorders', *British Columbia Journal of Special Education* 19: 11–19.

Hartas, D. (2004) 'Teacher and speech/language therapist collaboration: being equal and achieving a common goal', *Child Language Teaching and Therapy* 20 (1): 33–54.

Hegarty, S. (2004) 'Managing innovations in ICT: issues for staff development', in L. Florian and S. Hegarty (eds), *ICT and Special Educational Needs. A Tool for Inclusion*. New York and Buckingham: McGraw-Hill/Open University Press, pp. 128–45.

Ingram, D. (1969) 'Language development in children', in H. Fraser and W. O'Donnell (eds) *Applied Linguistics and the Teaching of English*. London: Longman.

Kamhi, A. and Catts, H. (1989) *Reading Disabilities: A Developmental Language Perspective*. Boston, MA: College-Hill.

Karmiloff, K. and Karmiloff-Smith, A. (2002) *Pathways to Language: From Fetus to Adolescent*. Cambridge, MA: Harvard University Press.

Law, J., Lindsay, G., Peacey, N., Gascoigne, M., Soloff,

N., Radford, J., Band, S. and Fitzerald, L. (2000) *Provision for Children with Speech and Language Needs in England and Wales: Facilitating Communication between Education and Health Services.* London: Department for Education and Employment.

Law, J., Lindsay, G., Peacey, N., Gascoigne, M., Soloff, N., Radford, J. and Band, S. (2001). 'Facilitating communication between education and health Services: the provision for children with speech and language needs', *British Journal of Special Education* 28 (3): 133–8.

Lees, J. and Urwin, S. (1997) *Children with Language Disorders* (2nd edn). London: Whurr.

McDonough, K. M. (1989) 'Analysis of the expressive language characteristics of emotionally handicapped students in social interactions', *Behavioral Disorders* 14: 127–49.

Martlew, M. (1992) 'Handwriting and spelling: dyslexic children's abilities compared with children of the same chronological age and younger children of the same spelling level', *British Journal of Educational Psychology* 62: 375–90.

Mosley, J. (1996) *Quality Circle Time in the Primary Classroom*, Vol. 1. London: LDA.

National Association for Language Development in the Curriculum (NALDIC) Working Group (1998) *Provision in Literacy Hours for Pupils Learning English as an Additional Language.* Watford: NALDIC.

Oakhill, J. and Garnham, A. (1989) *Becoming a Skilled Reader.* Oxford: Basil Blackwell.

Pappas, C., Kiefer, B. and Levstik, L. (1995) *An Integrated Language Perspective in the Elementary School. Theory into Action.* New York: Longman.

Prizant, B. M. (1991) 'Socioemotional aspects of communication disorders in young children', a short course presented at the annual convention of the American Speech Language Hearing Association, Atlanta, GA.

Prizant, B. M., Audet, L. R., Burke, G. M., Hummel, L. J., Maher, S. R., and Theodore, G. (1990) 'Communication disorders and emotional/behavioral disorders in children and adolescents', *Journal of Speech and Hearing Disorders* 55: 179–92.

QCA (Qualifications and Curriculum Authority) (2000) *A Language in Common: Assessing English as a Second Language*. London: QCA.

Raban, B. and Ure, C. (2000) 'Early literacy – a government concern'?, *Early Years* 20 (2): 47–56.

Raphael, T. E. and McMahon, S. I. (1994) 'Book club: an alternative framework for reading instruction', *Reading Teacher* 48: 102–16.

Stackhouse, J., Wells, B. and Murphy, N. (2004) 'Children's speech and literacy difficulties – a psycholinguistic framework' (review), *First Language*: 241–2.

Torgesen, J. K. (March 1996) 'Prevention and remediation of reading disabilities', paper presented at the Spectrum of Developmental Disabilities XVIII, Baltimore, MD: Johns Hopkins University.

Torgesen, J. K., Wagner, R. K. and Rashotte, C. A. (1994) 'Longitudinal studies of phonological processing and reading', *Journal of Learning Disabilities* 27: 276–86.

Vygotsky, L. S. (1962) *Thought and Language*. Cambridge, MA: MIT Press.

Watson, L. (1996) *Hearing Impairment*. Tamworth: NASEN.

Webster, A. and Wood, D. (1989), *Children with Hearing Difficulties*. London: Cassell.

Wells, G. (1986) *The Meaning Makers: Children Learning Language and Using Language to Learn*. Portsmouth, NH: Heinemann.

Westby, C. (1999) 'Assessment of pragmatic competence in children with psychiatric disorders', in D. Rogers-Adkinson and P. Griffith (eds) *Communication Disorders and Children with Psychiatric and Behavioural Disorders*. San Diego, CA: Singular.

Whitehead, M. (2002) *Developing Language and Literacy with Young Children*. London: Paul Chapman.

Woolfolk, A. E. (1998) *Educational Psychology*, 7th edn. London: Allyn & Bacon.